GOFFMAN
AND THE
MEDIA

Theory and Media

GOFFMAN AND THE MEDIA

PETER LUNT

polity

Copyright © Peter Lunt 2025

The right of Peter Lunt to be identified as Author of this Work has been
asserted in accordance with the UK Copyright, Designs and Patents Act 1988.

First published in 2025 by Polity Press

Polity Press
65 Bridge Street
Cambridge CB2 1UR, UK

Polity Press
111 River Street
Hoboken, NJ 07030, USA

ISBN-13: 978-0-7456-8888-6
ISBN-13: 978-0-7456-8889-3 (pb)

A catalogue record for this book is available from the British Library.

Library of Congress Control Number: 2023937101

Typeset in 10.75 on 14pt Janson Text LT Std by
Cheshire Typesetting Ltd, Cuddington, Cheshire
Printed and bound in Great Britain by CPI Group (UK) Ltd, Croydon

The publisher has used its best endeavours to ensure that the URLs for external
websites referred to in this book are correct and active at the time of going to
press. However, the publisher has no responsibility for the websites and can
make no guarantee that a site will remain live or that the content is or will
remain appropriate.

Every effort has been made to trace all copyright holders, but if any have been
overlooked the publisher will be pleased to include any necessary credits in any
subsequent reprint or edition.

For further information on Polity, visit our website:
politybooks.com

CONTENTS

ACKNOWLEDGEMENTS

This book has taken me far too long to write and I would like to thank all those colleagues, friends and family members who have continued to encourage the project and to talk with me, sometimes just to listen to me talk about Goffman. I've gained many insights and ideas from discussing the ideas behind this book and hearing other perspectives on Goffman's work from colleagues in media and communication over the years.

In the early stages of writing the book, I was fortunate to be part of a writing group consisting of Sonia Livingstone, Shani Orgad, Ellen Helsper, Lilie Chouliaraki and Bart Cammaerts, who read and commented on each other's developing draft chapters as critical friends. I am indebted to Jeff Pooley for his insightful and critical reading of an earlier draft of the book. I have very good memories of discussing Goffman's work as part of the Ross Priory group which helped shape the very idea of this book. I also benefited from the engagement of my PhD students who took up Goffman's work – especially Shuhan Chen, who I joined in writing the book *Chinese Social Media*, influenced by Goffman's analysis of face-work. On a longer timescale, my interest in how media scholars engage with ideas from Goffman's writings was stimulated by a book that Sonia Livingstone and I wrote as long ago as 1994 – *Talk on Television*.

I am grateful for the patience and support of the Polity publishing team, especially Mary Savigar, who has steered me safely towards publication in recent years. Thanks for your patience and support, Mary. I am grateful for financial support from the University of Leicester in the final stages of the manuscript's preparation. I am also very grateful for editorial support from Andrew Schrock, Dawn Rushen and Tim Clark for their excellent help and advice as copy-editors.

I would like to dedicate this book to the memory of Rodney Livingstone, with whom I had many interesting discussions as the book developed, and who would have been both surprised and delighted to see it finished, and to Sonia Livingstone for talking to me about Goffman among other things since 1981 and for making my life wonderful.

1

THE RECEPTION OF GOFFMAN'S WORK IN MEDIA AND COMMUNICATION

INTRODUCTION

This book explores the reception in media studies of the work of the sociologist Erving Goffman, from the era of mass communication to the current digital media age. Over a long history from the 1950s, Goffman's work has been influential in the study of interpersonal and mass communication, and has had something of a renaissance in the short past of studies of digital media. Paradoxically, given his influence on media studies, Goffman's work focused on the study of social interaction in everyday, face-to-face encounters; he wrote very little about the media and, in his early work, seemed sceptical about the potential of mediated interaction compared to the richness of copresent social interaction. Initially, his work and ideas were influential in the study of interpersonal communication and sociolinguistics. For example, his observations of how participants in social interaction used a variety of ways of signalling deference and creating conditions of civility and conviviality were taken up in socio-linguistics and developed into a systematic study of politeness (Goffman, 1967; Brown and Levison, 1987; Winkin and Leeds-Hurwitz, 2013). More surprising has been the influence of his work on the study of, first, mass communication from the 1970s and, more recently, digital and social media, given that Goffman valorized copresent, face-to-face interaction as a dynamic, nuanced, creative form of social action through which people realized their social identities, established and sustained social relationships, and contributed to social integration. Yet, as we will see, his work has translated well to the study of mediated social interaction and the interactional affordances of digital media.

In this book, I aim to answer the question of why Goffman's work has currency in studies of media and communication, and to explore the questions that arise from applying concepts and analyses derived from the study of face-to-face interaction to mediated social interaction. One reason, I will argue, for the continuing relevance of his work is that although Goffman's empirical research focused on the observation and analysis of social interaction in everyday life contexts, he was convinced that patterns of social interaction generated social order that complemented other forms of social order, such as those that are found in institutions and cultural forms. While he regarded the interaction order as an autonomous form of social order to be studied through microanalysis (Rawls, 2012), he also believed that interaction orders were ubiquitous in social life and played crucial roles in other forms of social integration (Giddens, 1984). Imagine an institution devoid of social interaction, for example. Goffman thought of the interaction order as operating within other social orders; although he did not theorize the relationship between social integration achieved through social interaction and the ordering of social systems, he made numerous observations concerning the role of interaction orders achieved through interaction in copresent social encounters, and framed his studies of social interaction in the context of a range of social theories. In this book, we will see how media researchers have taken up ideas from Goffman's work to examine two questions: what are the characteristics of mediated social interaction, and how are these played out in relation to media as a sociotechnical system (Brubaker, 2020)?

Goffman (1959, 1983) also believed that social interaction was significant because it played an essential role in various sociological processes, including self-formation, conformity as a secondary adjustment to social norms, social recognition and civility, and strategic interaction. He also believed that social interaction and the interaction order were implicated in social metaprocesses such as forms of public order, regions of social life and individualization. However, although he had these ambitions for the micro-sociological study of social interaction, Goffman did not develop a sociological theory. Instead, in the books produced over his long career, he sought to understand the social implications of interaction from various sociological perspectives and to demonstrate the macro-sociological implications of his analyses of interaction orders, and by implication address sociological questions such as the relationship between structure and agency. For example, Goffman studied the role of ritual in social life, the relation between phenomenology and sociology, the dynamics of framing, the relation between cultural forms such as the theatre and the performance of the self in everyday life, social exclusion as it arose in social interaction, and the characteristics of behaviour in public places. These engagements with sociological theories and processes link Goffman's studies of social interaction to questions of social influence and power, norms and individualization, even though he did not explicitly theorize these questions.

Goffman was skilled in formulating his observations and interpretations in powerful, evocative and valid concepts that captured the contexts, forms and dynamics of social interactions while pointing to broader social processes and structures. Many of the concepts coined by Goffman have become part of the analytic lexicon of the social sciences as well as being taken up in media studies. Self-presentation, impression management, performance, the distinction between frontstage and backstage, front, setting, ritual forms of social interactions, face-work, deference and demeanour, stigma, asylums as total institutions, relations in public, strategic interaction, focal and peripheral dimensions of social interaction, civil inattention, frames, keying and footing – these are all concepts that Goffman either coined himself or brought to the attention of communication scholars. As we will see throughout this book, they have proved to be a valuable resource in the study of media and communication, illustrating how we coordinate our engagements with others in social life, express and become our social selves, influence others and engage them in reciprocal and cooperative interaction, experience intersubjectivity in relationships and groups, enact our social roles, and generate local social orders that contribute to social solidarity while enabling individuals and groups to realize their purposes and aims.

These manifold social behaviours are also understood by Goffman to contribute to or to constitute social processes, including responses to social constraints, the relation between structure and agency, conformity and individualization. His analyses also recognize the many constraints on how people interact in everyday life, including social norms, civility, morality and etiquette, and the respect others have the right to expect in social encounters, all of which shape the form and dynamics of social interaction. At the same time, he recognized that social interaction created unique opportunities for participants to express themselves, explore their social identities, develop and sustain social relationships, persuade or influence others or bring them to account, and engage in cooperative, intersubjective experiences to thereby shape the situations in which they participated.

Goffman also recognized that although social interactions were a taken-for-granted part of everyday life, managing them was a skilled accomplishment in the context of dynamic face-to-face encounters in which participants had access to multiple channels of communication, including the proximity of bodies, non-verbal communication, being able to watch and monitor each other's conduct, and engaging in conversation, negotiation or shared experience. Another important distinction in Goffman's work was the contrast between rules expressed as constraints and creative rule-following in the dynamics of social encounters, through which he recognized the rule-governed and constitutive nature of the interactive order. In order to grasp these nuances and dynamics of social interaction in the concrete contexts of social encounters, Goffman approached the study of social interaction as a participant observer in which he aimed to capture the different forms of interaction in which people presented themselves to others, coordinated their actions and conversations, enacted their social and occupational roles, sought to understand each other, realized their aims and shared experiences across the myriad of contexts and circumstances in which social encounters occurred.

Consequently, when media researchers adapt concepts from Goffman, they buy into concepts that go beyond the summary of patterns of social interaction to engage these broader sociological themes and questions. I address the appropriation of Goffman's work in media studies in three ways: by exploring the potential of mediated social interaction, especially in the context of the interactional affordances of digital media, to qualify Goffman's focus on face-to-face interaction and scepticism towards mediated social interaction (Chapter 3); by exploring how Goffman's work has been linked to media theory and sociological questions in media studies (Chapter 4); and by exploring how it resonates with themes in contemporary, sociologically informed media research into media rituals, mediatization, media as practice, media phenomenology and the interdisciplinary relationships between media studies and sociology (Waisbord, 2014) (Chapter 5).

Throughout the book, two trends in the adoption of Goffman's concepts in media studies are addressed. First, there has been an emphasis on the analysis of self-presentation as performance derived from his first book, *The Presentation of Self in Everyday Life* (1959), and comparatively little work addressing his analyses of ritual and face-work (1955, 1956), social exclusion (1961, 1963a), behaviour in public places (1963b) and strategic interaction (1969). In addition, when self-presentation is studied in media contexts, the focus is often on impression management and the playing of information games by individuals seeking to persuade or influence others by projecting an image of the self, to the neglect of processes of social interaction, its reciprocal forms and intersubjectivity. A related tendency is the comparative neglect of Goffman's conception of self-formation as reflecting mutual recognition, cooperation and intersubjectivity in contrast to the pursuit of self-interest through social interaction. Also somewhat overlooked is Goffman's understanding of social interaction as a constitutive practice through which identities and social categories are formed and modified and social solidarity and social orders established; that is, the relation between social and systems integration (Giddens, 1984). This is particularly important given the mediation of everything (Livingstone, 2009) in which social lives and relationships are played out in the context of sociotechnical media systems.

In contrast to the many claims that Goffman eschewed explicit theory development, I place significance here on his implicit acknowledgement of an eclectic range of social theories. For example, a crucial influence on his work was Durkheim's (1984 [1893]) social psychology, which emphasized the plurality and diversity of modern life in which social solidarity could emerge through ritual, social encounters in everyday life, complementing collective forms of representation that reinforced social norms and moral values. His understanding of the self, as realized in the process of social interaction, was informed by Mead's (1934) distinction between the 'I' as a reaction to others' expressions and orientations towards the person and the 'me' as a consolidated set of beliefs and dispositions, as well as by Durkheim's (2005 [1914]) duality of the self, which combined elements of purposive, strategic forms of identity with social identity realized through intersubjectivity and participation in social practices. These ideas raise interesting challenges to analyses of individualization as a form of strategic rationality (Beck and Beck-Gernsheim, 2002). This view of social action as realized through interaction was written in contention with Weber's (1968 [1922]) analysis of modernity as increasingly dominated by rationalization processes, and Parsons's (1937) view of social action as structured through the authority of social norms and shared cultural values. In other words, adopting Goffman's concepts has a duality that points towards the contexts, dynamics and forms of social interaction in concrete social situations and to some of the essential themes and debates within sociology.

GOFFMAN AND MEDIA STUDIES

Goffman's work first came to the attention of media researchers between the 1950s and the 1970s. At that time, the field was divided between the study of mass communication and of interpersonal communication (Peters, 1999; Peters and Simonson, 2004). In interpersonal communication, and the related discipline of sociolinguistics, Goffman's work provided insights and concepts that inspired systematic developments in the field (Winkin and Leeds-Hurwitz, 2013). For example, the study of politeness was partly inspired by Goffman's (1967) analysis of how, through ritual acknowledgement and compliments, in greetings and compliments, participants in social interaction treated each other with respect, deference and civility. Brown and Levinson (1987) took Goffman's interpretations of patterns of civility in everyday life and developed a systematic approach to politeness, establishing it as an area of study. Winkin and Leeds-Hurwitz (2013) also documented how Goffman's work was taken up in mass communication research. For example, Goffman's (1974) concept of 'framing' has provided the impetus and inspiration for extensive media framing studies from the 1970s to the present (Winkin and Leeds-Hurwitz, 2013; Persson, 2022). His insights have enabled media researchers to develop approaches to analysing how information is 'framed' in media reports or programmes through selection, emphasis and narrative forms that often favour dominant or hegemonic perspectives – as discussed in Chapter 4, along with other examples of the application of Goffman's ideas in the study of mass communication.

Digital and social media blur the boundaries between interpersonal and mass communication, putting the capacity to reach potentially vast social networks into the hands of individuals, and enabling the development of digital spaces constituted through users' interactions. These developments have led to a resurgence of interest in Goffman's work in the study of the mediation of social interaction and the emergence of new forms of public life generated by interactions in networks of connectivity (Papacharissi, 2015). Significantly, the interactional affordances of digital media contrast with the limitations of the media technologies of Goffman's day. Goffman (1959, 1967) contrasted the subtle and dynamic properties of copresent, face-to-face interaction as a paradigmatic context for social interaction with the relatively restricted forms of interactivity of, for example, telephone conversation, and he was also sceptical about the potential for interactivity of mass communication as a one-to-many form of communication that did not afford dialogic forms of social interaction, which now proliferate in the age of digital and social media (Thompson, 1995, 2018). The development of mobile, digital and social media affords interaction at a distance that incorporates various channels of communication, includes visual and auditory cues, and affords simultaneity and interactional formations beyond the dyad, as we will see throughout this book. Goffman could only conceive characteristics of social interaction that afforded the constitution of interaction orders and their social effects as being possible in encounters played out as copresent, face-to-face social interaction, whereas crucial aspects of his analysis of social interaction are now accessible through digital media.

THE CONTEXT OF GOFFMAN'S WORK

A further paradox in the enthusiasm for Goffman's work in the context of contemporary studies of digital media arises because his work was embedded in his time – the United States from the 1950s to the 1970s – and reflects the intellectual context of mid-twentieth-century American sociology

(Calhoun, 2007; Giddens, 2009). Goffman (1963b) often suggested that the interactions he observed and interpreted were framed by middle-class, Anglo-American culture in the historical circumstances of the post-war period of the 1950s and early 1960s, notable for the expansion of consumer society, suburbanization and the rise of the middle classes against a background of international and internal tensions related to the Cold War, generating a contradiction between the growing affluence and access to material culture and a conformist political culture facing the existential threat of nuclear destruction, creating unease and emerging cultural resistance (Gitlin, 1987; Gaddis, 2006; Jaworski, 2022).

While he lived through turbulent times and witnessed radical developments in social and cultural theory, Goffman's normative project reflected the reformist politics of the progressive movement, as adopted by the Chicago School of Sociology (Bulmer, 1984), combined with liberal humanist assumptions, represented by Durkheim's (1995 [1912]) late work on the sociology of religion, law and politics. These commitments went against the grain of the mainstream sociology of his day, particularly Parsons's (1937, 1951) structural functionalism, which, partly in the service of national reconstruction, viewed social order and consensus as achieved in the complex, pluralistic society of the United States by legitimate authority combined with 'voluntaristic' conformity to established norms and values. In contrast, Goffman developed a subtle, 'outsider' questioning of how social controls and institutional contexts occluded the potential of human action and agency through which individuals might make a difference in their social world. In a sense, at least until the mid-1960s, Goffman was part of an intellectual counterculture (Gitlin, 1987), which found its voice in his criticism of the sociology of deviance and his focus on systemic forms of social exclusion and authority as social control in *Asylums* (1961a) and *Stigma* (1963a).

Over his career, Goffman became increasingly out of tune with the radical politics and critical social theory that emerged in the late 1960s. Whereas he once appeared 'cool' as part of a counterculture promoting a reformist agenda, his work seemed increasingly out of step with the more explicit focus on social structures, questions of power and radical social change that emerged in the 1960s (Mills, 1967; Gouldner, 1970; Calhoun, 2007). Within sociology, the perception of Goffman's work shifted from praise for its subtle questioning of social norms and values to its being regarded as mapping, and thereby reinforcing, the ideology of the emerging middle classes at a time of growing inequality, conflict and political conformity (Gouldner, 1970). In addition, Goffman's 'casual' approach to observation and interpretation and his essayistic writing style were criticized by those who claimed to take a more systematic approach to studying social interaction in ethnomethodology (Garfinkel, 1967) and sociolinguistic theory (see, for example, Brown and Levinson, 1987, on politeness).

Goffman's preference for empirical observation and antipathy towards explicit theory also looked increasingly problematic by the late 1960s, in contrast to the emerging approaches of ethnomethodology (Garfinkel, 1967), the social construction of reality (Berger and Luckmann, 1966) and critical social theory (Calhoun, 2007). Goffman's writing also used what would now be regarded as sexist or racist language. Although sensitive to forms of social exclusion (Goffman, 1963a; Rawls, 2022), his lack of sensitivity to the diversity of human experience and his apparent aversion to the politics of protest and social movements, compounded by his essayistic style and frequent use of irony, evoked a sense of privilege. More recently, in contrast, there has been an attempt to rehabilitate Goffman's work, including close (re)readings of his texts against the background of resurgent interest in his work in sociology (Jacobsen and Smith, 2022), where a contemporary Goffman (Jacobsen, 2010) is being rediscovered.

THE RECEPTION OF GOFFMAN IN SOCIOLOGY

Goffman is much more highly cited among sociologists today than during his career in the 1970s. Given the extensive secondary literature on his work (see Jacobsen, 2010; Jacobsen and Smith, 2022), and the manifold adaptions and extensions of his ideas in sociology and media studies, how can we now read Goffman? Jacobsen (2010) encourages us to continue to read Goffman in new ways and to link his work to innovations and revisions of sociological theory, to which we could add media theory. However, an acknowledged challenge in making sense of Goffman's work is its lack of explicit theoretical and conceptual development and the eclecticism of his sources, which makes it difficult to align his position with a single sociological theory or tradition. Indeed, Goffman has been classified as a symbolic interactionist, functionalist, structuralist, existentialist, phenomenologist, critical theorist and postmodernist (Jacobsen and Kristiansen, 2010). Jacobsen and Kristiansen (2010) argue that although Goffman's work overlaps with these traditions, he only partially signed up for some of them.

For example, Goffman's work is often aligned with his contemporaries at the Chicago School of Sociology, the symbolic interactionists (Blumer, 1992 [1969]; Rock, 1979). Aspects of his work are compatible with Plummer's account of the 'four interweaving themes' (2000, p. 223) shared by the various approaches to symbolic interactionism. First, human beings are capable of language and the use of symbols, which means that their social worlds are infused with meaning-making, through which people define and account for themselves and the situations they are part of in social interaction. The capacity to produce and share meanings enables them 'to produce a history, a culture, and very intricate webs of communication' (Plummer, 2000, p. 223). Consequently, although societies and institutions look stable, they are continually being renegotiated and reformed: 'In the world of the interactionist, meaning is never fixed and immutable; rather, it is always shifting, emergent, and ultimately ambiguous' (Plummer, 2000, p. 224). Plummer's second theme focuses on everyday life as a process in which social identities, lives, situations and even societies constantly emerge, evolve and adjust in processes of becoming. Third, symbolic interactionists think of social processes as sitting between society and individuals, so that the central unit of social analysis is interaction, understood as the core process through which the relationship between social processes, structures and individuals is constructed. Consequently, what can appear as fixed features of social life, such as roles, rules of engagement, established routines or moral principles, are open to adjustment or transformation during social interaction. Plummer's fourth theme is that symbolic interactionism focuses on empirical research rather than abstract social theory, coupled with the idea that social interaction is endemic and, therefore, a part of all aspects of the social world, be it a playground, café or boardroom.

Goffman shared these broad assumptions with symbolic interactionism. However, substantial differences set him apart from the various versions of this tradition. For example, his engagement with Durkheim's sociology is significant. In his study of routine forms of recognition and civility, Goffman defined his project as an application of Durkheim's social psychology to the study of everyday life of the United

States in the 1950s – in particular, Durkheim's (1995 [1912]) book on the sociology of religion which was based on a critical reconstruction of the social anthropological record of the lives of Indigenous Australians in the nineteenth century. Goffman adapted Durkheim's arguments about the soul and the sacred nature of human beings as articulated in positive and negative religious rites, which he saw as reproduced in the everyday courtesies and deferences involved in social encounters. Durkheim, especially as he had been interpreted by Parsons (1937), was a target of the symbolic interactionists partly because he had attempted to establish sociology as a positive science, in contrast to their interpretive sociology, and because he had sought to develop a theory of social structures and processes rather than an empirical study of social interaction. Goffman was also influenced by Simmel (1950) on the relationship between emergent patterns of interaction and established social and cultural forms; Durkheim (1995 [1912]) on the complexities of modern, pluralist societies and the sociology of religion, law and democratic political institutions; Weber (1968 [1922]) on strategic action; Mead (1934) on the social self; and Schutz (1967) on social phenomenology and the structure of the lifeworld and multiple realities.

The eclecticism of these sources is reflected in Collins's (1994) placement of Goffman's work in two sociological traditions: the Durkheimian tradition and micro-interactionism. In the Durkheimian tradition, Goffman sits within the lineage of social anthropology in his embrace of the moral basis of social life, the importance of symbolism, the organization of social interaction as ritual, and the cult of the individual. In the micro-interactionist tradition, Goffman inherited the pragmatist dimension of the Chicago tradition in the work of Peirce (2012), Cooley (1922) and Mead (1934), in synergy with Blumer's (1992 [1969]) symbolic interactionism and in dialogue with ethnomethodology (Garfinkel, 1967). Goffman is equally embedded in these somewhat contradictory positions within sociology, leading to a radical eclecticism and claims of a lack of theory development in his work (Jacobsen, 2010).

Goffman inherited many of these sources from the Chicago School of Sociology (Bulmer, 1984) and its creative synthesis of a reformist normative research programme and the philosophy of pragmatism (Misak, 2013). The Chicago School emphasized empirical research in the form of ethnographic study of how people resolved the challenges of living in modern urban society in the context of the disruptions and dislocations typified by the city of Chicago at the start of the twentieth century (Duneier et al., 2014). A key method adopted was urban ethnography, which aimed to develop detailed descriptions of the process of social life using an eclectic set of research methods combined with a sensibility to the practical problems of everyday life, or, as Anderson put it in *The Hobo*, 'How individual and collective agents go about dealing with the problematic situations they confront; the forms of practical reasoning they use; the habits, techniques, and attitudes they develop individually and collectively; and the feedback effects of these situations' (1923, p. 196). For Goffman, the paradigmatic context and means of managing the pressures of modern life was social interaction.

While neither pragmatism nor Chicago sociology were unified doctrines, the core themes of their work were influential on the young Goffman, shaping his normative project, his approach to empirical research and the way he engaged theories and developed concepts. Goffman believed that human beings were best understood as immersed in language and culture, and that intersubjectivity and social interaction affording reciprocal and coordinated social action were central to human self-consciousness and being in the social world (Mead, 1934). The pragmatist inheritance also influenced the idea that questions of social being are best understood through participant observation, and that the meaning and morals of actions depend on and constitute the definition of the situation in which they occur (Park et al., 1967 [1925]).

GOFFMAN'S RESEARCH PROJECT

How can we make sense of Goffman's work? In the final chapter of *The Presentation of Self in Everyday Life* (1959), Goffman recognized that in addition to his analysis of the interaction order there were alternative concepts of social order in sociology, which he characterized as technical, political, structural and cultural social orders. He argued that social interaction was not merely an alternative source of social order and cohesion, but that it was an essential part of all these forms of social order. He therefore treated his account of the interaction order as one of many perspectives on social order which together constituted a picture of modernity. He did not think any of the existing traditions of sociological theory constituted an adequate or complete understanding of modern society or had grasped the importance of social interaction to the integration of social systems (Giddens, 1984).

The core of Goffman's research and writing was the empirical project of the microanalysis of social interaction in everyday life. He explored self-presentation as performance, ritual forms of interaction as face-work and civility, social exclusion in institutional and everyday life settings, behaviour in public places and strategic interaction. Significantly, he used different sociological perspectives to frame these various empirical studies, thereby hoping to demonstrate the relevance and value of the interaction order across different sociological traditions. For example, he adopted Durkheim's (1995 [1912]) sociology of religion as a framework for his empirical investigation of social interaction as a form of recognition and respect of self and others. In his study of self-presentation as performance (1959) he was influenced by Simmel's (1950) analysis of the relationship between proto forms of social interaction in everyday life and established cultural forms such as the theatre, and in his study of self-formation through social interaction he followed Mead (1934). Through critical engagement with the sociology of deviance, Goffman analysed strategies of stigmatization through social interaction (1963a) and social control in the mental asylum (1961a). He also addressed role theory (Merton, 1957) in his analysis of how role distance was articulated in social interaction (Goffman, 1967; Pinch, 2010). In *Strategic Interaction* (1969) he provided a critical reconstruction of action theory, incorporating social interaction (Jaworski, 2022) in the context of developments in game theory and rational choice theory, and investigated the interactionist foundation of the organization of play and games as social practices. He also engaged Schutz's (1967) social phenomenology as well as ordinary language philosophy (Austin, 1962; Wittgenstein, 1953) in his analysis of the role of interpretive frameworks in guiding action and making sense of the social world.

Goffman's work, therefore, consisted of a series of case studies that mapped the forms and dynamics of social interaction across different domains of social life, and demonstrated the relevance of social interaction to different sociological theories and traditions, illustrating their relevance and, by extension, the centrality of the interaction order to all aspects of modern society (Goffman, 1983). In this context, we can make sense of his much-criticized essayistic style (Giddens, 2009), as each 'essay' took a perspective drawn from an established sociological theory of modernity, which was then adopted to study forms of social interaction.

STRUCTURE OF THE BOOK

While engagement with Goffman's work among media scholars has been extensive, both historically, encompassing the age of linear media and the present digital age, and in the breadth of engagement with his writings, there has been a tendency to focus on his early work on self-presentation as performance, with less attention paid, albeit with notable exceptions, to his work on ritual, social exclusion, public behaviour, strategic interaction and the dynamics of forms of talk in framing experience. Even the applications of ideas from Goffman's study of the presentation of self in everyday life tend to focus on individual strategies of impression management rather than on the dynamics of social interaction and the dispersal of interaction orders across different forms of social order. The use of Goffman's ideas in the study of media has tended towards applications of the concepts developed in his micro-sociology rather than examining how he sought to link social interaction to broader social processes such as conformity, structure and agency, social integration and public conduct. Goffman's rich concepts have often been applied piecemeal, without considering the broader themes in his work. Chapter 2, therefore, aims to introduce the breadth of that work to media scholars as a foundation for the following accounts of mediated social interaction (Chapter 3), engagements with the sociological themes in applications of Goffman's work in media studies (Chapter 4), and the relevance of his writings to contemporary media research and the relationship between media studies and sociology (Chapter 5). Goffman's work connects with several conceptual developments and debates in media and communication, including media phenomenology (Markham and Rodgers, 2017), understanding media rituals (Couldry, 2002), media and social practice (Bräuchler and Postill, 2010) and mediatization (Hepp, 2020). It also raises questions about self-formation in the digital age, the relation between powerful media and agency, and the interdisciplinary relationship between media and sociology (examined in Chapter 5).

The book ends with reflections on the widespread adoption of Goffman's sociology in the study of media and communication as an interdisciplinary practice that combines digital media and sociological analysis of late modernity, as reflected in themes in media research that explore the relationship between self-formation and media as a sociotechnical system.

2

GOFFMAN'S WORK: THEMES OF
COMMUNICATION AND MEDIA

INTRODUCTION

Chapters 3 and 4 provide analyses of studies of mediated social interaction and engagement with media and sociological theories in relation to Goffman's writings on the relation between structure and agency and the role of social interaction in social solidarity. However, in addition to a considerable literature on media studies influenced by Goffman, there is an extensive secondary literature within sociology on his work that has also been influential in the adoption of his ideas in media and communication. Furthermore, many of the applications of Goffman's concepts in the study of the media are somewhat dissociated from the context of his work and his empirical, theoretical and normative commitments. In this chapter, therefore, I introduce Goffman's ideas, focusing on the potential implications for media and communication research and taking into account how his ideas have been interpreted in sociology. This will provide a context for the reviews of applications of his work in the study of mediated social interaction and in relation to sociological themes and questions in media sociology in Chapters 3 and 4. The chapter reviews Goffman's writings from his work on the interaction order in *The Presentation of Self in Everyday Life* (1959) and *Interaction Ritual* (1967), the application of his analysis of social interaction to the study of social exclusion in *Asylums* (1961a) and *Stigma* (1963a), his books *Behaviour in Public Places* (1963b), *Strategic Interaction* (1969) and *Frame Analysis* (1974), to his later work on gender representations (1979) and the sociology of language in *Forms of Talk* (1981).

DRAMATURGY: THE PRESENTATION OF SELF IN EVERYDAY LIFE

Self-presentation as performance

Goffman is most well known for his work on self-presentation in social interaction as performance in the encounters of everyday life. This work was part of his PhD (2022 [1953]) and formed the basis for his first book, *The Presentation of Self in Everyday Life* (1959). Significantly, while developing his account of how social interaction was organized according to dramaturgical principles, Goffman (1955, 1956) also developed an analysis of social interaction ritual. The juxtaposition of these investigations into performance and ritual provides a broader context for understanding Goffman's account of social interaction and his understanding of the role of interaction in self-formation and civility. Taken together, drama and ritual address two dimensions of the social self: purposive social interaction in the form of persuasive performance and its dynamic relationship to mutuality and cooperation, and ritual interactions that constitute an environment that sustains social standing by recognizing

common humanity and cooperating in constructing reciprocal forms of social interaction and civility.

In his PhD, Goffman conducted a participant observation
study of social interaction in the Scottish island community
of Shetland. He would 'hang out' in public places such as
a hotel bar or restaurant, attend events such as dances, and
sometimes accept invitations to visit people at home. His
PhD was influenced by the tradition of urban ethnography
that developed in the interdisciplinary environment of the
Chicago School of Sociology (Bulmer, 1984). The Chicago
School had strong associations with the progressive political movement in the early twentieth-century United States;
it was committed to social reform and using academic
research to expose the challenging conditions of life in the
rapidly expanding city of Chicago. Although influenced by
this tradition, Goffman's study was neither a work of social
anthropology, as we discover little about social relations,
structures or processes on the island, and nor was it an urban
ethnography.

Broadly speaking, Goffman was interested in how
people used their interactions with others in everyday
social encounters to manage their lives in modern society
(Giddens, 1990). His primary unit of observation and analysis was social encounters, which occur whenever two or more
people gather or meet in everyday life. He aimed to understand how people organized encounters in such a way as to
be able to present themselves and manage civil engagements
with others. Performance is how we project an image of ourselves and communicate our inner thoughts and feelings to
others in social encounters. In contrast, ritual focuses more
on caring for the self and creating the conditions for civility.

In developing his analysis of self-presentation as performance, Goffman searched for functional equivalents between
how performances are organized in the theatre and how they

are organized in everyday social encounters. Theatrical performances are organized through scripting, staging, rehearsal and character presentation in front of an audience in a space of performance: the frontstage. In the backstage, actors prepare themselves for their onstage performance. In everyday encounters, people take turns, address others, coordinate speech and action, open and close conversations and seek to make a positive impression on others. Significantly, in this analysis, Goffman was comparing the established cultural form of the theatre with the informal organization of performance in everyday life.

For example, the theatre is a specially constructed performance space with a stage and seats for the audience; it thereby separates performers and audience, fixing their social roles and restricting their access to specific regions of the theatre. In contrast, the performance of the self in everyday life occurs in living rooms, offices and coffee shops, and participants take turns at being performers or audiences. Theatres have props, scenery, lighting and make-up departments, whereas the performance of self in everyday life makes use of whatever is to hand, such as 'furniture, décor, physical layout and other background items which supply the scenery and stage props for the spate of human action played out before, within or upon it' (Goffman, 1959, p. 22). Theatrical performers are dressed and made up in character, whereas in everyday life participants make use of their bodies, clothing and conduct to construct a 'personal front' that includes 'insignia of rank; clothing, sex, age, and racial characteristics; size and looks; posture; speech patterns; facial expressions; bodily gestures; and the like' (Goffman, 1959, p. 22). Theatrical performances are rehearsed, and actors prepare by warming up, putting on their costumes and applying make-up; the stage is set, the lighting planned, the curtain raised for the performance in front of an audience, and the play unfolds as a sequence of scenes organized into acts. Everyday social encounters have some of these elements – for example, they have openings and closings and people play different interactional and social roles within them – but most interactions in social encounters have a sense of liveness and flexibility and offer the freedom to people to influence the unfolding of interactions rather than follow a script.

Another contrast is that the theatre audience recognizes that the part an actor plays is fictional, their words usually written by an author rather than being the actor's own or representative of their personal identity. In contrast, in everyday life, people typically perform themselves or their social roles, raising different questions about truthfulness and authenticity. Goffman draws our attention to the different communication roles in social encounters. In the theatre, actors use their acting skills to give a credible and arresting performance of their character across the unfolding scenes of the play in collaboration with their fellow performers. The audience also reacts appropriately to the onstage action by laughing, gasping or watching silently, and by applauding at the end.

While performance in the theatre commonly follows a script, everyday social encounters are more spontaneous and constructed on the fly. However, Goffman recognized a form of 'scripting' in everyday life, as when an 'individual will already have a fair idea of what modesty, deference, or righteous indignation looks like, and can pass at playing these bits when necessary' (1959, p. 79). In addition to this repertoire of dramatic cameos, some social encounters follow a conventional schema as a sequence of actions or routines, like the plot of a play divided into acts and scenes. For example, eating in a restaurant involves booking a table, travelling to the restaurant, being greeted and seated, looking at the menu, ordering, eating and paying the bill: the conventions of eating in a restaurant thus follow a script.

Goffman developed his analysis of how social roles were performed in everyday life, illustrating this through an example from Sartre (1956) that captures the performance of the waiter's role. Sartre noticed the obsequiousness of the waiter's bodily orientation towards diners, his demeanour, expressions and mode of address. What is the waiter doing? 'He is playing, he is amusing himself. But what is he playing? We need not watch for long before we can explain it: he is playing at being a waiter in a café' (Goffman, 1959, p. 82). Goffman explored how waiters, wrestlers, con artists and spies included theatrical elements in their self-presentations. A wrestling match is organized based on an agreement between the fighters on sequences of action, on who will play the roles of the bad guy and the straight guy, and on which falls and manoeuvres will be used in the fight. In this context, 'the details of the expressions and movements used do not come from a script but from command of an idiom, a command that is exercised from moment to moment with little calculation or forethought' (Goffman, 1959, p. 80).

In contrast to the professionalism of theatrical performance, everyday self-presentation is performed by reflexively aware but flawed participants, so that 'the impression of reality fostered by performance is a delicate, fragile thing that can be shattered by minor mishaps' (Goffman, 1959, p. 58). Managing the fragility of self-presentation is part of the practice and skill required in everyday life. In addition, participants can observe each other and check the validity of each other's self-presentations, providing a powerful constraint on self-presentation. For example, participants can potentially see when someone makes an explicit claim about feeling confident as information is given, in contrast to expressions of nervousness in non-verbal communication as information is given off. However, just as an actor can use their theatrical skills to portray an emotion that is not their own, in everyday life people can 'feign' emotions and exploit common-sense assumptions about which emotional expressions are controllable and which are not. Nevertheless, this control over the expression of feelings is not complete, in contrast to an actor's skill in performance. Consequently, in everyday life, in the dynamic interplay of social interaction, participants can undermine their attempt at self-presentation as feelings that might contradict the image they are trying to portray leak out. As we will see, this leaking of private information in public is a feature of the digital media environment.

Goffman identified several normative conventions that govern expectations for the self's performance in everyday life. We expect ourselves and others to present the self in the best light, truthfully, consistently and orientated to the cooperative effort of others in defining the situation. We expect ourselves to be observant, bring other participants to account, say what we are entitled to say, and not deceive fellow participants.

In all this, Goffman understood performance as a communicative process of making our feelings and thoughts visible through 'dramatic realization', analogous to the way an actor realizes their character through dramatic performance: 'For if the individual's activity is to become significant to others, he must mobilize his activity so that it expresses *during the interaction* what he wishes to convey' (1959, p. 40; emphasis added).

Teams

Up to this point, Goffman had mainly referred to the interaction between dyadic pairs of speakers/hearers in the pragmatic roles of performer/audience. However, many social encounters involve groups of participants, which changes the communication framework and complicates the roles people play in social interaction. Goffman considered how this impacted self-presentation, and how people work together to support and protect the image portrayed by individuals or the group. Teamwork establishes 'a bond of reciprocal dependence linking teammates to one another' (Goffman, 1959, p. 88). Team members follow rules that guide teamwork, such as avoiding disagreement in public, disclosing information to teammates, and maintaining the party line during performances as a display of dramaturgical loyalty. Team members must also exercise self-control (dramaturgical circumspection) to project a positive image. In this way, Goffman brought our attention to the work that participants, sometimes not the focus of attention, do to sustain self-presentations made by team members. The conditions of possibility for self-presentation require the support of others present in the social encounter.

Compared to the rehearsed and skilful performances of a troupe of actors on stage, team performances in everyday life are fragile and can be discredited, disrupted or rendered useless. However, various defensive practices have developed by which team members can mitigate these threats through information control. For example, they can prevent audiences from gaining access to evidence that might discredit or undermine the image or definition of the situation projected by the group: 'a team must be able to keep its secrets and have its secrets kept' (Goffman, 1959, p. 141). Goffman offered examples of control of self-disclosure in group contexts, in relation to dark secrets, which potentially undermine the image the team is trying to project, and strategic secrets that keep the team's intentions and self-presentational strategy secret from others, reducing potential resistance and disruption. Insider secrets are those shared by group members, tying them together. There is also a phenomenology of group experience in play. Team members attempt to remain attentive and disciplined and will employ social skills to 'stay cool' if something goes wrong or if there is a threat to identity.

Goffman also identified 'discrepant roles' that can support or undermine the team. An informer may sell out the team by revealing its secrets to the audience. A shill pretends to be an audience member to encourage support for the team, or agents sit in the audience and complain about the performance while pretending to be neutral. Goffman developed the idea of communicative roles in social encounters through these examples. At any given moment in a group interaction, not everyone is the focus of the encounter; some participants are peripheral but still play a role. Only some people in a social encounter can speak as a 'ratified' participant. In a restaurant, for example, diners at the same table are ratified participants in and the focus of the conversation around the table; those on adjacent tables, although they can overhear the conversation, are expected to demonstrate civil inattention and politely ignore, or appear to ignore, what they overhear. These ideas of communication roles and the social relationships adopted in social interaction were later developed in Goffman's (1981) work on 'footing'.

Regions and region behaviour as frontstage and backstage

In his participant observation studies, Goffman (1959) observed that the interactions between waiters and diners differed from those between waiters and chefs in the kitchen area. Adopting the distinction between the frontstage and backstage areas of the theatre, Goffman suggested that the dining room was the setting for the performance of the waiter role, while backstage in the kitchen, the waiters did not need to perform their roles and could adopt a more relaxed interactional style. The distinction between frontstage and backstage areas in the theatre is marked by barriers to access and different expectations of how to behave in these regions. In the hotel, diners are confined to the dining room, the chefs and kitchen hands to the kitchen, but waiters must navigate the transition between front and back regions. For Goffman, this represented a crucial feature of the organization of experience in social life: that people routinely make transitions between spaces that demand quite different performances and interactional styles, a version of the phenomenological concept of *epoche*, or being able to shift routinely between different orders of social reality. Goffman also suggested that the distinction between the space of performance and the backstage of informal or familiar social relations represented a general cultural tendency in which, 'throughout Western society, there tends to be one informal or backstage language of behaviour, and another language of behaviour for occasions when a performance is being presented' (1959, p. 128). A crucial feature of the mediation of everyday life is that the media transcends or blurs these distinctions in social life, connecting people across time and place, and making many things that were once private publicly available. Copresence is expanded in space and time, and the distinctions between public and private are blurred. The implications of this will be discussed later, in Chapters 3 and 4.

The arts of impression management

Goffman is often interpreted as providing a view of social interaction as cynical and manipulative, as if the performance of self-presentation is separate from an internal authentic self. However, while he acknowledged that social interaction could serve strategic aims or be used to influence or manipulate others, he also recognized that strategies of impression management had other functions in everyday social encounters, such as managing the fragility of social interaction and creating the conditions for reciprocal social engagements. For example, he observed commonplace strategies used to deal with or avoid ways in which unmeant gestures, inopportune intrusions or gaffes might disrupt a social scene, leading to potential embarrassment. The skilful deployment of the arts of impression management requires exercising discretion, avoiding disrupting social encounters, being mindful of potential threats to the impression the group is trying to project, and intervening when necessary to distract, cover up or recover from problems. There are also a variety of practices through which those present in a social encounter create the conditions for reciprocity by exercising control over their personal feelings, displaying poise under pressure and being sensitive to shifts in the affective climate of the encounter. Such protective practices are as much the responsibility of audiences as performers, who can support, laugh or engage at appropriate moments and, above all, avoid making a scene.

A feature of Goffman's work is the sense that there is a normative expectation that people in social encounters should avoid disruption and seek harmony or equilibrium in their interactions with others. This theme in his analysis of the interaction order has been interpreted in different ways, including the idea that he supported a conservative form of social life where people conformed to norms of politeness, or that such strategies were a contribution to public order, for example, as a form of civil inattention (Geuss, 2001): 'In middle-class Anglo-American society, when in a public place, one is supposed to keep one's nose out of other people's activity and go about one's own business', which constitutes for middle-class people 'the walls which effectively insulate them' (Goffman, 1959, p. 224).

Conclusions to The Presentation of Self in Everyday Life

In the conclusions to *The Presentation of Self in Everyday Life*, Goffman emphasized that dramaturgy, the analysis of self-presentation as performance, was only one of several possible perspectives on the interaction order. Goffman himself was already exploring ritual as a way of organizing interactions in social encounters at the time he was working on dramaturgy, and he would go on to research interactional strategies to manage social exclusion, social encounters as games, strategic forms of social interaction, and the organization of experience through frameworks of interpretation including communication frameworks. The idea that there are different ways in which social encounters are organized in everyday life is significant when set against the preoccupation with self-presentation as performance in the secondary literature and the take-up of Goffman's work in media studies. While acknowledging the relevance of self-presentation in mediated social interaction, this book will explore how other perspectives on the interaction order are taken up in media and communication (in Chapters 3 and 4).

Goffman (1959) also discussed possible links between the interaction order and other forms of organizational or institutional social order, such as the technical, political, structural and cultural. The technical view of social institutions is exemplified by bureaucracy, which focuses on rationally organized activity systems oriented to goals. The political view of social establishments examines the relative power of individuals or groups over others within an organizational setting. The structural view of social establishments concerns horizontal and vertical status divisions, while cultural order refers to social relations between groups within an organization. A critical suggestion that Goffman made was that the interaction order was implicated in these other forms of social ordering such that structures and processes of social institutions were partly constituted through the interactions between members and participants. Power relations are often, although not exclusively, mediated through social interaction. Cultures, including organizational cultures, are partly constituted through practices in which social interactions play a crucial role. Significantly, the various examples Goffman provided in his account of the performance of self-presentation as mediated through social interactions provide a foothold for agency as collaborative action in institutional and cultural forms and social systems. Although Goffman (1983) felt that he had yet to persuade his fellow sociologists of this idea, it remains one of the reasons why media scholars are attracted to his work as they contemplate the role of agency in increasingly mediated societies.

In linking, albeit casually, interaction orders with other sociological accounts of social order, Goffman pointed to the relationship between the performance of self-presentation in everyday life and macro-social structures and processes that are paradigmatic of the relationship between structure and agency. What appears to be a metaphor for everyday drama is a relationship between micro and macro, as the organization of theatrical performance is the rationalization of practices of self-presentation in everyday life, which also provides resources for the presentation of self. In addition, the processes, rules and structures that characterize social institutions are often enacted through social interactions, bringing the interaction order into play within established social and cultural forms. Social interaction constitutes a kind of shadow order, creating regions in the interstices of social structures that play an essential role in institutional organization. Goffman suggested that sociological accounts must consider the interaction order in their explanations of social life.

The Presentation of Self in Everyday Life ends with reflections on the self as performed in and constituted through the interaction order, which picks up on the idea that self-formation plays a crucial role in linking agency and structure: 'The self, then, is a performed character, is not an organic thing that has a specific location, whose fundamental fate is to be born, to mature, and to die; it is a dramatic effect arising from a sense that is presented, and the characteristic issue, the crucial concern, is whether it will be credited or discredited' (Goffman, 1959, pp. 252–3).

SOCIAL LIFE AS RITUAL: DEFERENCE, DEMEANOUR AND FACE-WORK

Significantly, Goffman was working on the idea of ritual as a form of organization of interactions in social encounters while developing his account of self-presentation as performance. In a sense, he considered the ritual organization of social interaction as the antithesis of self-presentation as performance. As we have seen, in self-presentation there is a tension between a strategy of projecting an image and cooperative forms of social interaction that coordinate action or constitute forms of reciprocity. Goffman claimed that different conceptions of the self were realized through social interaction, for example in strategic self-interest and cooperation. In his work on ritual forms of interaction in social encounters, he explored how participants created and protected the conditions for recognizing others' humanity and constituted a context for care of the self.

In 'The nature of deference and demeanor' (1956) and 'On face-work' (1955), Goffman explored the 'little salutations, compliments, and apologies which punctuate social discourse' (1967, p. 57). He interpreted everyday civility in social encounters as the result of ritual practices that created conditions in which mutual respect was realized. Referencing the Chinese conception of 'face' in terms of reputation based on achievement (*mianzi*) and standing in the community (*lian*) (see Chen and Lunt, 2021), Goffman looked at how reputation as 'face' emerged in social interaction as the product of participant actions and interactions. Like self-presentation, face is inherently fragile, so people can find themselves in the 'wrong face' or 'out of face'. This can result from not having a way of being or acting in a social situation, where, in a dramaturgical sense, a person has no line to take, leading to a lack of confidence and disorientation.

In contrast, being 'in face' produces confidence, a sense of security and relief. In social encounters, threats to face are commonplace, and various strategies have been developed to manage them. For example, participants can alleviate the effects of threats to face by demonstrating poise under pressure, using social skills or diplomacy. Protective manoeuvres are also used to anticipate and avoid potential threats, such as showing respect and politeness, displaying courtesy, acting with discretion, avoiding potentially challenging topics and employing circumlocution to preserve face (Goffman, 1967). Even when the best attempts by participants to save face fail, several fall-back strategies can be deployed, such as pretending that the problem did not happen (tactful blindness), acknowledging the event but denying that it is a challenge to face, or pausing and turning aside for a moment to allow participants to collect themselves. These actions and forms of interaction simultaneously create a supportive environment and display a respect that reinforces individuals' sense of self.

In his essay on deference and demeanour, Goffman (1956) offered a theoretical framing for face-work by interpreting everyday rituals from the perspective of Durkheim's conception of social identity and the sociology of religion. Durkheim identified a duality in social identity between our strategic selves in which we seek to maximize our interests through our relationships with others and those aspects of ourselves realized through the mutual recognition of our common humanity in reciprocal, collaborative social relations of civility. In his analysis of the anthropological record of religious practice in Indigenous Australian tribes and clans, Durkheim (1995 [1912]) focused on totemic religion in which, through ceremony, the clan worships or honours an object or animal that becomes the symbol of the clan. In addition to its crucial role in ceremonies, the totem was recognized in everyday practice through rites that determined rules of access to it and the appropriate behaviour in its presence. In applying these ideas to modernity, Durkheim argued that the individual is treated as a sacred object and recognized as sharing a common humanity, creating organic solidarity based on civility in conduct between individuals. This contrasts with the collective form of mechanical social solidarity constituted through shared experience of ceremony. Both symbolize the clan or society through the totem of a deity or the sacred individual. Goffman applied these ideas from Durkheim's social psychology to everyday ritual forms of interaction as forms of recognition, civil inattention and politeness. These niceties of respect and civility recognize our common humanity and constitute a form of mutual recognition: 'If persons have a universal human nature, they themselves are not to be looked to for an explanation of it. One must look rather to the fact that societies everywhere, if they are to be societies, must mobilize their members as self-regulating participants in social encounters. One way of mobilizing the individual for this purpose is through ritual' (Goffman, 1967, p. 44).

These rituals complement Goffman's analysis of the organization of social interaction as the performance of self-presentation. Goffman argued that everyday rituals constituted the interaction order through interactions that recognized the sacredness of the individual and symbolized a society based on human rights law and democratic institutions. As social interaction now increasingly occurs in digital media environments and through social media, we will examine in Chapters 3 and 4 how self-presentation and ritual are played out in mediated contexts.

THE SOCIOLOGY OF DEVIANCE: ASYLUMS AND STIGMA

Goffman's studies of self-presentation and ritual provide insights into the role of social interaction in self-formation, social solidarity, the enactment of social roles and the coordination of actions in everyday life contexts through examples that are mostly interactions between relatively equal partners. In his bestselling book *Asylums*, Goffman (1961a) examined the mental asylum as a total institution that controls the life of inmates so that social interaction, self-formation and sociality are heavily constrained. Asylums sequestrate individuals from their everyday lives and control their social behaviour. Goffman complemented his study of social control over social interaction in an asylum with a study on stigma (1963a) as a form of constraint operating through social interaction in everyday contexts as a form of social exclusion. In contrast with his previous studies of social interaction, these studies invite the question of what happens to the agency and freedom associated with self-presentation and mutual recognition through ritual forms of civility in the face of social control and stigmatization. They also point to the broader political culture of the United States in the 1950s and 1960s in the context of fears associated with the Cold War and a potential nuclear holocaust. Goffman's social control and exclusion studies challenged Parsons's (1951) analysis of the relation between authority and voluntary conformity, and how this structured social action. They also have implications for theories of media as powerful institutions that shape people's lives and as a context in which stigma as social exclusion plays out.

Asylums

Following his PhD, Goffman obtained a research position on a project to conduct a participant observation study of the life of inmates on a ward in a mental asylum. At the time of his study in the early 1960s, there was a broad life politics movement challenging psychiatry, the medical model of mental illness and the institutional control and management of the lives of people with mental health conditions. Szasz's *The Myth of Mental Illness* (1961), Foucault's critique of psychiatry in *Madness and Civilization* (1964) and Laing's *The Divided Self* (1960) all raised awareness of the potential injustice of the incarceration of those labelled as mentally ill, challenged the validity of psychiatric diagnosis and identified asylums as instruments of social control in the guise of therapy. These ideas were also represented in popular culture, for example in Kesey's (1962) novel *One Flew Over the Cuckoo's Nest*. Goffman's contribution was to analyse the mental asylum as a total institution that controlled and constrained inmates' behaviour in contrast to the relative freedoms of everyday social life.

Goffman began with a discussion of the forms of total institutions, such as prisons and asylums, as regions of life with relatively impermeable boundaries 'often built right into the physical plant, such as locked doors, high walls, barbed wire, cliffs, water, forests or moors' (1961a, pp. 15–16). Within the walls of a total institution, inmates are treated uniformly under a single and robust regime of authority. Access to and from the asylum is controlled, and inmates generally live out all facets of their lives within its walls. Entry into the asylum is rarely the first step in what Goffman termed a mental health career, arguing that patients were 'funnelled' into diagnosis or self-diagnosis by family, friends, coworkers and various medical and health professionals. In other words, social exclusion in everyday life precedes medical diagnosis, bringing into question the idea that patients voluntarily accept the role of the patient.

On entry into the asylum, people are stripped of clothing and personal insignia, depriving them of their 'personal front' through a process that Goffman described as being 'disinfected of identifications' (1961a, p. 16). Such institutions have established routines in which everyone does everything together. Bedtime is determined by lights out, and routines are enforced by officials such as jailors or psychiatric nurses, reflecting an overarching rationale or 'official' plan (Goffman, 1961a, p. 17). Total institutions establish control for no apparent purpose except to create a sense of order and discipline. Compared to social interaction as drama and ritual, the asylum removes the respect, dignity, recognition and freedom typically afforded to individuals in everyday social encounters. The capacity to give and receive respect in collaborative relations with others is severely restricted. Institutionalized social exclusion involves the withdrawal of social support, the loss of autonomy, the reduction of opportunities for intersubjectivity and the removal of rights, which Goffman (1967) regarded as defining features of social being.

Despite these examples, Goffman stopped short of arguing that the asylum constituted a totalizing system of control. He documented inmates' strategies and tactics to manage their self-identity even in this unpromising context (de Certeau, 1984); for example, patients engage with staff using their interpersonal skills to subvert the system of institutional privilege; others practice 'playing it cool', biding their time to mitigate the effects of life in the total institution (Goffman, 1961a, pp. 60–65). Some adopt a strategy of 'strategic withdrawal', limiting their horizon of experience to reduce the adverse effects of engagement, at the risk of institutionalization, 'regression', 'prison psychosis' and 'acute depersonalization' (Goffman, 1961a, p. 61). Occasionally, inmates adopt an 'intransigent line' by challenging the institution or openly refusing to cooperate with staff (p. 62). This is common among new inmates and is met by an institutional response that includes solitary confinement, drug therapy or electric convulsive treatment (ECT) to break their resistance. Goffman also identified a 'conversion' strategy through which inmates modelled themselves on staff, adopting their language, clothing and attitudes towards other inmates.

Goffman's perspective and sympathies were mainly with the inmates; however, he recognized the contradictory position of staff working in total institutions caught between social control and medical treatment, reflecting two forms of talk in 'people work' and 'object work' (1961a, p. 73). He argued that psychiatry objectified patients as a problem and implemented a penal system of social control through restraint and punishment in the name of treatment.

Goffman compared the life of the asylum inmate to accounts of Nazi concentration camp survivors. Kogon's *The Theory and Practice of Hell* (1950) and Cohen's *Human Behavior in the Concentration Camp* (1953), both written by social scientists who were camp survivors, reflected on the individual's vulnerability in the face of overwhelming authority. Goffman aimed to understand the operation of coercive power in a space sequestrated from everyday life in a culture that reflected many of the characteristics of premodern society, such as a penal code of discipline and punishment rather than restitutive law, minimal role differentiation among inmates, and being subject to a regime of sovereign power (Foucault, 1979). The rise of powerful media corporations raises similar concerns about constraining choice, limiting options and surveillance, which we will discuss later in Chapter 5.

Stigma

Asylums are a metaphor for problems of surveillance and control as instruments of power in the context of a free society, and throw into relief the freedoms that Goffman identified in social interaction in everyday life (1961a). In his analysis of stigma (1963a), Goffman extended his investigation of the role of social interaction in relation to social exclusion outside of the asylum. He examined routine social exclusion in everyday social encounters from the perspective of stigmatized people and their strategies to manage their potentially 'spoiled identities'. Goffman regarded stigma as formed, maintained and resisted 'in social relations between people and [social] categories' rather than being 'a property of the stigmatized attribute itself' (quoted in Hannem, 2022, p. 52). Stigmata are physical signs or behaviours that mark a person as 'different' based on a socially devalued attribute. Goffman recognized that different attributes could be used as the basis for stigmatization, including physical deformities, failings of moral character, and identifications of race, religion and class. He also recognized the arbitrariness and cultural variation of the attributes identified, and that stigmatization was not determined by the attributes but by social exclusion. Goffman did not explain why particular attributes were identified in a given society at a given historical moment, and offered little comparative evidence for his views (Tyler, 2020). His focus was on how stigma played out in social interactions and the strategies used by those stigmatized to manage the process of social exclusion. *Stigma* brackets out questions of how and why particular attributes are stigmatized, and the social, cultural and power dynamics behind this process (Goffman, 1963a).

Goffman's analysis focused on the process of stigmatization and the strategies developed by those affected to avoid or mitigate its effects. He illustrated the strategies used to manage a spoiled identity with the dramatic case of a girl born without a nose and therefore deprived of a face in a literal and potentially humiliating sense, which brought attention to the individual as deviating from the norm. He was interested in the range of strategies the girl used to manage her 'spoiled identity' and thereby ameliorate the potential consequence of being socially excluded. She used various forms of concealment and countered or defused comments about her condition in social interactions. Goffman pointed out that the effortless mastery of social life that 'normals' enjoyed was unavailable to her and, by extension, to all who bore a mark of being different and were thereby subject to routine social exclusion in everyday life.

In contrast to visible stigma, some stigmatized attributes are not visible, in which case individuals are potentially 'discreditable'. People can avoid being discredited by controlling information and keeping the attribute a secret. This draws on Goffman's analysis of the distinction between information 'given' and information 'given off' in social interaction. Invisible marks of stigma can be managed because they are, to a degree, under the individual's control. In contrast, visible marks of stigmatized attributes are less under the control of the stigmatized person and are given off in social interaction. Goffman recognized stigmatization in everyday social action, and here we are interested in how these processes change through mediation.

Criticisms of Goffman's work on stigma suggest that his focus on social exclusion in everyday life failed 'to adequately attend to the impact of inequality, power, and institutions in interactions between the stigmatised and the stigmatiser ... [that] shape everyday interactions' (Hannem, 2022, p. 51). While most of *Stigma* is a study of the interactional strategies and tactics adopted in the face of prejudice, towards the end of the book Goffman made some observations about social exclusion beyond the attempts of individuals to avoid labelling, particularly about the racial politics of his day, as this affected African Americans and gender stereotyping (Tyler, 2020). He acknowledged the various forms of stigmatization related to sexuality, gender, geopolitics and race, and identified a persona that stood for a norm as that of a youthful, married, white male from the north of the United States (see Tyler, 2020). Arguably, Goffman did not pay sufficient attention to the power relations, structural inequalities and structures of authority that rendered this ideal normative and that both caused and maintained social hierarchy through stigmatization. There are limits to what can be identified as a significant social process of social exclusion from the perspective of the microanalysis of social interaction (Tyler, 2020). Another consequence of Goffman's focus on episodes of stigmatization in social encounters is that it radically understates how the lived realities of both race and gender are not simply individual acts in occasional episodes but also the continuous effects of living in a society organized around racial and gender oppression or 'terrorism' (Tyler, 2020, p. 109). As Hannem (2022) argues, there is anecdotal evidence that Goffman was unwilling to engage with the more radical critical theory and life politics movements that emerged in the 1960s. The limits of interactionism in analysing social inequality and power are highly relevant to the adoption of Goffman's concepts in the study of the media, where questions of power and the role of media in everyday life raise similar questions, as will be discussed in Chapter 5.

BEHAVIOUR IN PUBLIC PLACES

A critical question that Goffman faced was that although his early work had established that everyday life was partially organized as local interaction orders, and had contributed significantly to the sociology of everyday life in raising awareness of how crucial self-formation was for understanding individualization, he had assumed, rather than demonstrated or argued, that these local orders constituted a form of social order that shaped modern societies. While there were hints and suggestions in his work and references to macro-sociological theories, notably Durkheim's (1995 [1912]) and Simmel's (1950) sociologies of culture and Parsons's (1937) sociology of action, he did not provide a theoretical analysis of the ways that interaction orders were embedded in and constituted societal processes or structures. Goffman addressed this question in his book *Behavior in Public Places* (1963b), which provided an interactional analysis of the relative orderliness of life in public in his society.

Goffman saw the taken-for-granted, relatively ordered engagements of people in public places as a phenomenon that required explanation. He also recognized the contrast between the focused interactions he had studied in relation to self-presentation and ritual and the largely unfocused forms of interaction among people in public places. He contrasted the constraints of the asylum on social interaction with the relative freedoms of public spaces. Such spaces were also, for the most part, relatively free of the molestation of stigmatization. This is not to say that there were no dangers and fears in participation in public life, far from it, but it brings to our attention how typical orderliness is in potentially risky situations of public gatherings of strangers. The kind of orderliness that prevails in public places varies. Compare those attending a football match, a concert, a lecture or a club. Although there are visible orders across these contexts, they each have their idiom of engagement and behaviour. Goffman sought, as he often did, to draw out the common elements of how behaviour in public places was organized through social interaction.

Goffman (1963b) identified the features of the ordering of behaviours in public places as situational propriety, involvement, accessibility and civil inattention (Manning, 1992; Smith, 2022). Situational propriety addresses how people adjust or attune their actions to the context of public gatherings. Involvement varies from being peripherally or loosely embedded to being engaged and focal to the occasion, signalled through 'attention displays' (Smith, 2022). Participants can signal their availability for interaction in public spaces, or their lack of availability by using objects such as newspapers or novels (or, nowadays, mobile phones) as 'involvement shields' (Ayaß, 2014). In addition, it is common for participants to share a focus while also adopting a secondary focus – as in going to a concert with friends. Civil inattention is accomplished by not drawing attention to ourselves in public, respecting others' personal space, and allowing them to get on with their own business as part of recognizing barriers and boundaries of involvement in the relatively open gatherings of public life (Geuss, 2001). These ideas provide a scheme for analysing constructed publicness and publics in the media and behaviours in the public places of social media (Livingstone, 2005).

STRATEGIC INTERACTION:
SOCIAL ENCOUNTERS AS GAMES

At various points in his analyses of how social encounters were organized as drama, ritual, stigma or orderly public conduct, Goffman referred to social encounters as games. This makes sense because, like social encounters, games are rule-governed social practices bounded in space and time, combining collaboration and competition and involving both individuals and teams, all of which had been included in Goffman's analyses of performance and ritual. Games also afford the potential to deploy and finesse skills and capabilities, an essential element of social practices (Bourdieu, 1977; MacIntyre, 1981). Games also vary, from informal play to organized, professional sports, reflecting Goffman's interest in the contrast between everyday social encounters and those in institutional contexts. There are other ways in which games are structured as exchanges. For example, playing tennis involves turn-taking moves, while team games require collaboration within the team and competition between teams. Games also combine elements of ceremony and ritual.

Considering social encounters as games enabled Goffman to explore the implications of sociological analysis of decision-making and strategic action for the interaction order. Rational choice theory (Abell, 1996) emphasizes the role of choice and decision-making in the pursuit of personal interests or preferences. In contrast, Goffman was in tune with significant developments in the mathematical theory of games, or game theory, exemplified by Simon's (1982) concept of 'bounded rationality'. Economists and mathematicians have developed sophisticated mathematical analyses of decision-making based on strong assumptions about decisions as rational choices, whereby agents act based on perfect knowledge and with unlimited decision-making capacity. In contrast, Simon's conception of bounded rationality recognizes that most practical decisions are made in conditions of uncertainty and are constrained by both the cognitive limitations of decision-makers and the limits on available information.

One game theorist who read Goffman's work, Schelling (1979 [1960]), identified different kinds of multiplayer games as forms of social exchange and aimed to understand the relationship between trust (cooperation) and risk (competition) in game playing (Manning, 1992, p. 61). Schelling argued that strategic bargaining was common in conflict situations and could be generalized to many real-world situations in organizations and to conflict in everyday social situations. Strategic bargaining requires understanding the perspective of other players and role-playing, and Goffman's analysis demonstrates how social interaction creates the conditions of possibility for strategic rationality. These ideas reflect Simmel's (1950) and Durkheim's (1995 [1912]) accounts of the non-contractual principles that create the contexts in which competition or exchange occurs. In team sports, players play competitively within the game's rules, without which competition would be unbounded.

Although strategic interaction is one of Goffman's many rich concepts that have been adopted in various social science disciplines, the book of that name was not well received by reviewers (Goffman, 1969; Jaworski, 2022), who questioned whether Goffman had added anything meaningful to his analysis in *The Presentation of Self in Everyday Life*. Jaworski (2022), however, argues that the book has value as a reflection on the conformist political culture of the 1950s and early 1960s. He also interprets Goffman's analysis of strategic interaction as continuing and refreshing the Chicago School tradition of linking insights from game theory to the analysis of social interaction. The game metaphor enabled Goffman to clarify the role of equilibrium as a crucial organizing principle of social encounters and a constraint on social interaction. In this, Goffman contrasted conformity with secondary adjustment as interactional conventions and patterns that provide a framework for expression and sociality. The idea of moves in a game also provided a way of thinking about the turn-taking and manoeuvres of participants in social interaction as elements in social practices. Finally, as games involve rules and creative forms of contest and collaboration, they add to an understanding of social practice as involving freedom within constraints. However, behind the reception of *Strategic Interaction* (1969), there was a growing discontent with Goffman's work and a shift in the intellectual climate that led to criticisms of his approach and of the normative value of his project.

CRITICAL RESPONSES TO GOFFMAN'S WORK

By the late 1960s, Goffman had produced an impressive body of work that included several bestselling books that were widely read and highly regarded within sociology and other academic disciplines, and by the general reading public. His work contributed to establishing social interactionism and micro-sociology as fields of study, helped to revitalize the Chicago tradition and challenged the dominant schools of sociology of his day. He asserted the importance of understanding social interaction for accounts of social action, social order, the character of public life and social exclusion. However, from the late 1960s, his work was increasingly criticized for a lack of rigour and systematicity in his empirical research methods and approach to analysis, a lack of theory development and avoidance of critical sociological questions such as social hierarchy, power, inequality and the analysis of social structures and processes. His implicit normative assumptions were also questioned as reflecting reformist

traditions in contrast to more critical and radical sociological approaches emerging in sociology in the United States in
his time (Calhoun, 2007). Where previously he had appeared
to be in tune with social and cultural critique, he was now
increasingly perceived as a conservative thinker out of step
with radical currents of theory, research and critique and
the life politics movements of the late 1960s and early 1970s
(Tyler, 2020).

Critical social theory was concerned with consumer-
ism and the alienating effects of suburbanization, while the
developing life politics movements focused on inequality and
identity politics. In this context, Goffman's analysis of everyday social interaction and social relations was interpreted
as revealing cynical and disinterested individuals engaged
in strategic social encounters. Goffman's work appeared
to reflect the ideology of an emerging class fraction in the
post-Second World War period in the United States, characterized by individualism, isolation from tradition, family and
community, and immersed in consumer culture (Gouldner,
1970). Gouldner's critique of Goffman was an influential and
widespread interpretation of his work as a masterful analysis
of social interaction that required the context of accounts of
social influence, power and structure to address sociological
questions. In addition, alternative sociological approaches
to analysing social interaction in everyday life emerged in
this period. Garfinkel's *Studies in Ethnomethodology* (1967)
and Berger and Luckmann's *The Social Construction of Reality*
(1966) provided highly influential accounts of the sociology
of everyday life.

The ethnomethodologists developed an alternative to
Goffman's approach to the study of naturally occurring
social interaction. They focused on analysing the capabilities of participants to make themselves intelligible based
on systematic analyses of recordings of naturally occur-

ring social interactions, capturing detail in real time, and developing an accountable transcription process for analysing naturally occurring interaction. In contrast, Goffman's approach to interpretation appeared unsystematic, weaving together evidence and interpretation to construct a narrative account of contexts, practices and forms of social interaction. Also, the emerging approach of social constructionism provided a more specific account of the relation between social interaction and social situations. For example, Berger and Luckmann (1966) linked practices to societal norms and values through processes of internalization and social construction in everyday life, potentially overcoming Goffman's focus on the forms of social interaction in social encounters with somewhat vague suggestions about their links and relevance to a macro-sociological analysis of social systems and structures.

FRAME ANALYSIS

Rather than provide a traditional academic response to his critics, in his book *Frame Analysis* (1974) Goffman instead attempted to reconstruct his work on the interaction order in light of their criticisms. One criticism had been of the need for theory development in Goffman's work, and the introductory chapter of *Frame Analysis* invokes various theories of the relationship between language and social practice that understand language and social reality as constituting maps with multiple regions or realities. Schutz's (1967) work on the structures of the lifeworld, James's (1950 [1890]) analysis of multiple realities, Wittgenstein's (1953) analysis of language games, Austin's (1962) work on speech acts and Barthes's (1972) semiotics provide a variety of perspectives. These sources all offer ways in which experience and language can be understood as integrated and organized in the context of a cultural form of life. As Persson suggests, in *Frame Analysis*, Goffman attempted to construct 'a sociology of multiple realities without falling into extreme social constructionism' (2022, p. 120).

Goffman's aim was 'to try to isolate some of the basic frameworks of interpretation available to our society for making sense out of events and to analyse the special vulnerabilities to which these frames of reference are subject' (1974, p. 10). Crucially, he understood frames not as fixed meaning structures but as realized through social practice and open to transformation. He referred to Bateson's (1973) analysis of play fighting among otters in a zoo, which identified the overlaps and nuanced differences between fighting and play fighting. If we take fighting as a starting point, then elements of that practice are retained in play fighting while other elements are transformed. For example, biting is replaced by nipping. Play fighting is a transformation of fighting so that the actions take on a different meaning and have different trajectories and material consequences. Frames create the background to our experience of social situations and our interactions with others; they provide a framework as a starting point for action and interaction while being open to transformation as an encounter unfolds.

Frames work on different levels of abstraction; Goffman suggested that, at the most abstract level, primary frameworks encoded fundamental cultural assumptions about the place of action in the material and social worlds as the paramount reality of human experience. Natural frames provide mechanical conceptions or models of the natural world used to make sense of occurrences that are 'undirected, unoriented, unanimated, unguided, "purely physical"' (Goffman, 1974, p. 22). However, natural frames do not exclude agency because 'intelligent agents can gear into the ongoing natural world and exploit its determinacy, providing only that the natural design is respected' (p. 23). In contrast, social frames are schemas that require human action and interaction to be realized. These frames represent fundamental assumptions about the material and social world we inhabit so that, 'taken together, the primary frameworks of a particular social group constitute a central element of its culture' (p. 27).

Goffman used geometric transformation to understand frame transformation, in which aspects of geometric form are retained when an object is rotated, flipped over or shifts position. In a similar way, musical transposition changes the key of a piece without affecting the melody or rhythm. Following this train of thought, Goffman identified ways of transforming frames through keying. In make-believe, frames are transformed through playfulness, daydreaming and dramatic scripting. In contests, strategies and modes of play can rekey the framing of the contest. Ceremonies simulate life or distil moments of life. In technical readings, an event is simulated in advance or afterwards, as in rehearsal, practice or recordings of events. 'Regroundings' use transformations to trick or deceive participants. In addition, multiple keyings and rekeyings are possible within a social encounter so that more than one transformation can be applied (a play within a play), which Goffman called 'lamination'. Within a social encounter, we can shift the embedding of different frames up and down through lamination. These arguments draw on Schutz's (1967) analysis of how, pragmatically, we move with ease across the boundaries between different forms of reality construction as a practical accomplishment.

Goffman offered a frame analytic interpretation of his earlier work on deceit and fabrication in self-presentation in which transformations persuaded participants into false beliefs about what was happening in a situation. Some fabrications are benign and playful; some are experimental or used to test friendship or loyalty. Other forms of fabrication

may be deployed, such as camouflage, mimicry or intimida-
tion, and can aim to exploit. Goffman also discussed the idea
of a 'theatrical frame' in which individuals were transformed
into stage performers through dramatic scriptings, lectures
or talks and work performances of various kinds. Audiences
are participants in these kinds of fabrications. He also used
the idea of lamination to rethink ideas from his analysis of
conventions for staging in the theatre and everyday life. The
stage, where the performance takes place, is marked at its
beginning by the physical separation between performers
and audience, curtains being drawn, prologues and a variety
of other theatrical conventions constituting 'an abrupt entry
into an alternative order of being' that has few parallels in
everyday life (Goffman, 1974, p. 138). During the play, the
performance is framed by the stage as a room with no ceiling
and one wall missing, thereby 'exposing doings' to the audience. The actors on stage present their interactions on the
half-turn oriented towards each other and in the direction
of the audience. The characters take turns to be the focus in
their relationship with other actors as their 'stage audience'
in the performance. Spaces are left in the action for audience participation. Several 'theatrical' devices, such as asides,
soliloquies and self-confession, acknowledge and draw in the
audience, so the latter become 'intimates of a world they are
not part of' (p. 142). As we will see in Chapter 3, the study of
mediated communication frameworks applies these ideas to
mediating social interaction.

Goffman (1974) also made some remarks on techniques
of framing and transformation in other forms of media. For
example, radio production uses various strategies to compensate for the lack of visual and non-verbal cues in radio
transmissions. He observed that, unlike naturally occurring
conversation, radio speech could not be 'distended', so radio
engineers developed techniques such as the spatial distribu-

tion and relative volume of microphones to create the sense of an auditory field to compensate for the lack of depth perception. Similarly, because we cannot smell, taste or feel on radio, various devices have been developed to compensate, including substituting sounds for visuals (a tweeting bird), verbal commentary (who is opening the door?), sound effects and music to create ambience. Finally, Goffman discussed how these compensations worked differently in different media: stage, theatre, cinema, television and novels. These strategies are not simulations of face-to-face interaction contexts but give the audience 'just enough' so that they can use their imaginations to experience the scene created by the screen, sound or image. These ideas were influential in the analysis of media events (Dayan and Katz, 1992).

Starting from the tension in the way frames of interpretation are structured as shared frames of reference or media frames, Persson (2022) argues that frames can be understood as incorporating three dimensions: cognitive, interactional and situational. The cognitive dimension refers to the framing of information, which has been the focus of much work on media framing (Benford and Snow, 2000), and which will be discussed in Chapter 4. Participants in social situations also use frames to coordinate their actions in the organization of experience. For example, the interactional dimension of framing specifies who is entitled to speak and in which voice, and frames the relations between participants as communication frameworks (Goffman, 1981). Although frames are linguistic and behavioural codes representing social facts, roles, relations and interactional forms, the realization of codes in concrete social situations opens them to transformation as they can be adapted, challenged or used for different purposes rather than being treated as formal rules (Persson, 2022).

In his subsequent publications, Goffman applied frame analysis to the study of gender representations in print advertising (1979) and the analysis of forms of talk (1981). The analysis of gender adverts and the 'Radio talk' essay in *Forms of Talk* represent Goffman's most explicit analysis of the media.

GENDER ADVERTISEMENTS

In *Gender Advertisements*, Goffman (1979) applied frame analysis to gender representation in print advertising. The book includes an introduction by Vivian Gornick, a feminist writer, journalist and advocate who recognized that Goffman's sensitivity to 'the most simple gesture, familiar ritual, a taken-for-granted form of address, has become a source of new understanding concerning relations between the sexes and the social forces at work behind these relations' (Goffman, 1979, p. vii).

What caught Goffman's attention in his analyses of gender advertisements was that pictorial advertising, as a cultural form, often depicted scenes from everyday life. He sought to understand the recursive relationship between media culture and everyday life whereby representations emerge from everyday practices, experiences and identities, and to provide modes of reflection on representations of social categories and power relations. Goffman started with the idea that adverts were ceremonial and provided 'the affirmation of basic social arrangements and the presentation of ultimate doctrines about man and the world' (1979, p. 1). Ceremonies also mark and solemnize key moments or junctures in people's lives, such as 'christenings, graduations, marriage ceremonies, and funerals', and frame the temporal organization of social life, as in the relation between ceremony, seasons and holidays. In the reception of adverts, 'the individual is allowed to face directly what he is supposed to hold dear, a presentation of the supposed ordering of his existence' (p. 1).

Goffman's central insight about the form of photographic adverts came from reflecting on portraits and pictures in art. In traditional portrait painting, 'the model sits or stands in his finery, holds an absent, half smiling expression on his face in the direction he is instructed to ... and renders himself up to the judgement of eternity' (1979, p. 16). Goffman suggested that early photographs followed the portrait format, partly because of the length of exposure required, so that the model had to hold their pose for a few seconds, and partly because cultural forms lag behind technical developments. The development of camera technology led to the convention of the snapshot in which models were arranged 'as if' caught during an activity in a mise-en-scène, often a social encounter, apparently unaware of being photographed. In this context, we, the audience, are put in the position of the overseer with our gaze focused on the photograph. This format produced 'natural' shots, which gave the impression of having grabbed a moment in a scene from everyday life.

Goffman analysed print adverts constructed as capturing moments in the unfolding routines of everyday life (ritual), as playful interactions (games) and as creative interactions (drama) that presented 'gender displays' of culturally shared views of sex differences. Hierarchical relationships are revealed in the portrayals of gendered behavioural styles, 'affirming the place that persons of the female sex-class have in the social structure, in other words, holding them to it'. This form of representation means that 'these modes of functioning are concealed from us by the doctrine of natural expression' (Goffman, 1979, p. 8). Photographic adverts use various techniques to present the unequal social status of men and women; for example, one 'way in which social weight – power, authority, rank, office, renown – is echoed expressively in social situations is through relative size, especially height' (p. 28). In groups of men, those with higher social or occupational status are taller in Adland. Counter-stereotypical examples portray women of higher social standing as taller than the men in the scene. Differences in height are reinforced by 'function ranking' in which men are typically placed in a position of higher social standing, such as a male doctor with a female nurse or a male coach with a female player. There are occasional humorous examples where men are put in the functionally dependent position, as in one advert with a man doing the laundry.

In Adland, women, as objects of the male gaze (Berger, 1972), are presented as emotionally expressive. For example, the feminine touch is illustrated by how a woman's hand frames objects of desire, holding and caressing them, tracing their outlines. The lightness of touch is emphasized and sometimes takes the form of self-touching of the face, mouth or hair. Women are often portrayed in a state of 'licensed withdrawal', in contrast to men, who are present, wide awake and ready to initiate or respond. Women are also often presented in a drifting, dreamlike, self-absorbed state, gazing into the middle distance, covering their faces with their hands or looking sideways.

Goffman identified in gender adverts a parent–child complex in which the man acts by empowering and acting in the woman's best interests in a gendered structure of care that gives the child permission to play, scream, cry and be naughty. Men, like parents, act with 'protective intercession', and the home becomes a space organized around the woman/child. In adverts, this model of dependency extends to gender relations where women are afforded 'indulgent proclivities' and men are often portrayed as protectors standing in the wings, giving licence to the woman, with the implication that the parent/man can intervene so that 'male domination is an exceptional kind, a domination that can be carried right into the gentlest, most loving moment without apparently causing strain' (Goffman, 1979, p. 8).

Many studies of gender advertisements have been conducted in social psychology and media and communication, and displays of mise-en-scène from everyday life are an essential aspect of digital and social media, which often present snapshots of everyday life.

FORMS OF TALK

Forms of Talk (1981) is a collection of essays in which Goffman addressed the criticism that he had an unsophisticated approach to language analysis. Three main themes are addressed across the collection: ritualization, participation frameworks and embedding. Ritualization refers to the conventional gestures established within a community. Participation frameworks organize the communicative roles people take up in a social encounter. Embedding refers to the contrast between communication roles and voice in which, 'although who speaks is situationally circumscribed, in whose name words are spoken is certainly not' (Goffman, 1981, p. 3).

The essay 'Radio talk' is Goffman's other piece focused on the media, in this case, the management of errors in radio DJs' otherwise smooth presentational style. Goffman was interested in the DJ's skill of providing an intimate, seemingly private voice while speaking in public to an unknown, unseen audience in which the DJ seeks to 'produce the effect of a spontaneous, fluent flow of words – if not a forceful, pleasing personality – under conditions that lay speakers would be unable to manage' (1981, p. 198). Albeit in a professionalized form, Goffman was interested in the competencies that lie behind the ability to hold a conversation, make an announcement, or the many other different forms of talk that are routinely accomplished and constitute the interaction order. He also picked up the theme of the contrast between professional performance and everyday life in a reworking of his previous accounts of the fragility of self-presentation and ritual, and the strategies adopted to deal with potential disruptions as these are managed in the practised hands of the DJ.

The central point that Goffman makes in 'Radio talk' is that the appearance of spontaneity, or fresh talk, requires a lot of planning, practice and skill. In a similar way to the actor portraying an emotion on stage, the DJ creates a sense of real, authentic self-presentation that is a performance. The competency of the DJ is to routinely accomplish this complex task without making production strategies visible to the listening public. As in Goffman's analysis of repair strategies in everyday social interactions that might cause embarrassment or loss of face, the DJ has to manage any mishaps or mistakes in performance without appearing to be doing so. In this context, Goffman distinguished between substantive forms of restitution, such as offering an apology, and ritualistic making good of the potential source of embarrassment. In this case, professionalization takes the ritual form of moving the conversation on without recognition of or reflection on the potential gaffe or mishap. Goffman also suggested that these practised forms of making good constituted an idiom realized in practice rather than a set of norms of conduct – they are realized in the flow of broadcasting. He identified several faults that could occur at any moment in the flow of speech from a DJ in a live performance: hesitations or stuttering as interruptions to the flow of language; slips, as in things mis-said, grammatical infelicities or errors of pronunciation; problems in understanding or grasp of the subject matter being discussed; and gaffes, or unintended bad manners or indiscretions. In everyday conversations, there is commonly an acknowledgement of the problem followed by a remedy. The DJ develops several devices to recognize and repair these breaches to ensure the smooth production of fresh talk. Critically, the DJ seeks to achieve this without shifting the relationship with the imagined listener so as not to disturb the footing on which their engagement is based. The professionalization of mediated self-presentation as reflected in the broadcasting of the self and influencers in social media is discussed in Chapter 4.

We now turn to the question of the orientation of participants in social interaction, or 'footing', as Goffman (1981) called it, in the analysis of communication frameworks. His essay 'Footing' starts with an example of breaking frame in the ritual signing of a bill by then-US President Richard Nixon. During the ceremony, Nixon commented on the appearance of a female journalist wearing trousers ('slacks'), and expressed the view that he hoped she would wear a dress next time and do a 'twirl'. With this intervention, Nixon objectifies the woman and addresses her in her domestic rather than professional role through an aside as 'small talk' bracketed off from the professional and formal framing of the occasion. Goffman analysed this code-switching as a shift in footing, which involves changes in the communication roles adopted in a social encounter. Shifts in footing involve 'significant shifts in alignment of speaker and hearers' (1981, p. 127).

Goffman argued that participants played various roles in communication frameworks. For example, a social encounter may have one 'speaker' and multiple 'hearers'. Hearers can be addressed as a group (as in the theatre) and sometimes divided into ratified and unratified. In a talk show interview, for instance, two people, the host and the guest, play out a speaker/hearer dialogue in front of an audience (Livingstone and Lunt, 1994). These positionings in a participation framework are open to transformation depending on who is speaking/in focus, and social situations vary in terms of how fluid the participation framework is. Participation frameworks assign people to different communication roles, identified by Goffman as those of principal, animator and author. A principal is 'someone whose beliefs have been told and who is committed to what the words say' (Goffman, 1981, p. 145). An animator provides the vocalization or a voice box for communication. The author scribes the words spoken by the animator and represents the principal's interests. Goffman's point here is to challenge a fundamental assumption of the speaker-hearer model: the speaker combines the roles of principal, animator and author.

GOFFMAN'S RECEPTION IN SOCIAL AND CULTURAL THEORY

In addition to the value of Goffman's concepts for media research and the links between his analysis of social interaction and a range of social questions, another reason for the continuing interest in and relevance of his thinking is the critical engagement it has received from social and cultural theorists whose work is influential in media studies. For example, Butler (1990) challenges Goffman's concept of performance, preferring that of performativity to understand how rituals and repetitions of gender categories in everyday social interaction objectify and reinforce those categories. Butler rejects Goffman's account of performance because it propounds a view of gender categories as expressions of inner gender identity analysed from an ethological perspective combined with a phenomenological analysis of experience. Butler links Goffman's dramaturgy to popular theories that reflect the imagination of gender prior to the 'acts, postures, and gestures by which it is dramatized and known' (1988,

p. 528). Goffman's dramaturgy is also interpreted as enacting social roles that express or disguise an interior gendered 'self' (Smith, 2010). Goffman is portrayed as representing a two-selves view of gender identity that propounds a myth of interiority and expression in contrast to the idea that gender categories are a 'publicly regulated and sanctioned form of essence fabrication' (Butler, 1988, p. 528).

Goffman's work also has much in common with Austin's (1962) speech act theory, in which meaning is understood as action in contexts guided by convention. Habermas (1984) drew on speech act theory in his analysis of the relation between reason and action as part of his theory of communicative action. Although he cited Goffman's (1959) dramaturgical analysis of self-presentation as performance as an alternative to strategic and normative forms of reason in action, Habermas focused on Goffman's analysis of how performance made mental states visible to other participants in social interaction, in contrast to his analysis of communicative action which aimed to achieve mutual understanding. MacIntyre (1981) examines the implicit moral theory in Goffman's analysis of self-presentation, concluding that it is an example of emotivism in which the meaning of moral statements is exhausted by their attempt to persuade others to accept the speaker's position, disguising their social and cultural assumptions. Giddens (1991a) links Goffman's work to the analysis of reflexive modernity and the realization of the project of the self. Developing this theme, Brubaker (2020) connects Goffman's work with Giddens's (1991a) and Foucault's (1978) concepts of the technology of the self and the care of the self, examining the role of digital connection in self-formation. These examples demonstrate that implicit in Goffman's work is an engagement with questions of meaning, action and intersubjectivity alongside questions of agency and structure, individualization, social influence and power, self-formation, the enactment of social roles and the constitution of social categories (Rawls, 2022). Even though Goffman rarely discussed such issues explicitly, his analyses of social interaction in everyday life invite an engagement with these fundamental questions in social and cultural theory. Such questions are highly relevant to media research focused on the analysis of performance/performativity in mediated social interaction, the contrast between constructing or expressing states and feelings, and the relation between structure and agency in mediation and mediated self-formation, as will be explored in Chapters 3, 4 and 5.

CONCLUSION

In the analysis of communication, Goffman's work provides a unique voice that 'straddles a number of disciplinary approaches and traditions – part sociology of interaction, part ethnography of speaking, part sociolinguistics of verbal performance' (Sidnell, 2022, p. 131). His empirical research combined observation and interpretation supplemented by illustrations from various cultural artefacts such as newspapers, novels, etiquette books and, as we have seen, advertisements. He lived in a world saturated with language in myriad forms, in which interaction in everyday social encounters was highly significant. His recognition of the social significance of everyday life is one of his achievements. His work is lauded for its nuanced analysis illustrating the different forms of social interaction constituting the inter-action order. While the core of his empirical project involved observing, interpreting and naming different forms of the interaction order as drama, ritual, game, stigma, frames and forms of talk, Goffman was also convinced that the inter-action order played a significant role in modern society as a context for the formation of the self, constituting social order through local interaction orders and public orders as an organic social solidarity made possible through social interaction. However, he was less successful at convincing his colleagues in sociology that he had explained the relationship between micro-sociological analysis of the interaction order and societal structures and processes.

Throughout this chapter, I have linked Goffman's work to questions in media and communication. In the following two chapters I will discuss examples of how media researchers have adopted ideas from Goffman's work in studies of the mediation of social interaction (Chapter 3), and the potential societal implications of research on mediated social interaction (Chapter 4). Chapter 3 explores whether the interactional affordances of digital and social media invite a revision of Goffman's distinction between face-to-face and mediated social interaction. Can we now talk about a mediated interaction order? Does the development of media technologies since Goffman's time create conditions that afford real-time, multichannel communication, the coordination and framing of social interaction, a sense of copresence, dynamic forms of social interaction, mutual observation and accountability, shared experience and intersubjectivity, communication frameworks and roles that simulate aspects of Goffman's account of the features of face-to-face social interaction? Does the enhanced interactivity of contemporary digital media create conditions where individuals can realize social identities and deploy self-presentation, and enable organic social solidarity, civility, recognition and mutual respect? Chapter 4 explores studies of media and communication that engage with Goffman's work for understanding the links between the interaction order and broader social structures, processes and cultures as a contribution to media sociology (Waisbord, 2014). In the final chapter, Goffman's work is linked to contemporary studies of mediation and mediatization, media rituals, media phenomenology and the relation between powerful media and agency, and the implications for thinking about the interdisciplinary relationship between media studies and sociology.

3

MEDIATED SOCIAL INTERACTION

INTRODUCTION

This chapter focuses on how Goffman's writing has inspired, informed and been adapted to the study of mediated social interaction. What follows is not an attempt at a comprehensive literature review but an analysis of examples of different ways in which Goffman's ideas have been taken up in the study of mediated interaction. The examples also range across time to encompass various means of technologically mediated social interaction, from linear to digital media, involving different communication forms and frameworks. Goffman valorized copresent, face-to-face social interaction in everyday encounters because it provided communication through multiple channels – aural, visual and non-verbal – and presupposed the proximity of bodies, creating an environment that maximized the dynamic qualities and responsiveness of interaction. This in turn afforded the potential for individuals to realize their social identities and sense of self, constitute and sustain social relationships, recognize others as social beings, achieve their aims, establish and defend their reputations, and contribute to social solidarity through the formation of the interaction order. In Goffman's view, copresence is an essential background for social interaction as it creates a rich communication environment by placing people close to one another, occupying the same space and time and social context, enabling them to coordinate their actions, optimize mutual accessibility, co-construct the meaning of a social situation and have a shared experience of intersubjectivity.

In comparison, interaction that involved the communication technologies available when Goffman was writing, such as the telephone, post or telegram, seemed to him to significantly diminish the affordances for social interaction, limiting the richness and subtlety of mediated interaction so that it reduced the capacity for individuals to realize their social beings and sustain social relationships compared to face-to-face interaction. In the 1950s and 1960s, when Goffman was developing his account of social interaction, the introduction and rapid diffusion of television in the United States as a popular form of one-to-many communication only reinforced his view of the limitations of mediated social interaction. He noted various production techniques deployed to compensate for the interactional limitations of mediated communication which draw our attention to the limits of mediated social interaction (Goffman, 1974). For example, radio sound engineers compensated for the lack of visual cues in a radio drama production by using sound effects, which included positioning microphones to create a sense of depth and ambience in the soundscape that simulates the visual field. Dayan and Katz (1992) used Goffman's idea of compensatory mechanisms in their analysis of media events, demonstrating how television coverage uses similar techniques to create a sense of being present for viewers remote from the event. However, Dayan and Katz also suggest that the media can give a view of live events that, in some ways, goes beyond what those physically present can experience, such as gaining a panoptic vision of the event, access to a variety of viewpoints, and commentary provided for the viewer, all of which enhance the experience of mediated live events.

Thus, there are two ways in which developing media technologies might overcome limitations arising from the lack of copresence in comparison with face-to-face communication: by simulating aspects of copresence or by augmenting mediated social interactions in ways that are different to the affordances of face-to-face contexts. This potential for simulation and augmentation has been radically extended by mobile and digital communication through the proliferation of the technological means for interaction at a distance and extended networks of connection (Hutchby, 2014): 'The digital age is distinguished by rapid transformations in the kinds of technological mediation through which we encounter one another. Face to face conversation, land-line telephone calls, and postal mail have been joined by email, mobile phone calls, text messaging, instant messaging, chat, web boards, social networks, photo sharing, video sharing, multiplayer gaming, and more' (Baym, 2015, p. 1). Consequently, digital media was 'immediately recognised as a complex medium of communication that incorporated elements of both interpersonal and mass communication' (Katz and Rice, 2002, p. 203).

Media researchers have found Goffman's writings to be a valuable resource in understanding the continually changing affordances of digital media. They have studied mediated self-presentation, impression management, ritual forms of interaction in media such as face-work, self-formation, copresence and communication frameworks in digital media contexts. A key question addressed by these studies is whether digital media technologies provide functional equivalents of the affordances of face-to-face social encounters or augment social interaction in ways unanticipated by Goffman. For example, do digital media create conditions where participants can share experiences or augment forms of visibility and gain access to different views or perspectives? Do the affordances of digital media enable new forms of coordination, collaboration and intersubjectivity? Finally, can digital media create communication frameworks in which participants can play out communicative roles and manage the 'footing' of their social interactions?

SELF-PRESENTATION ON PERSONAL HOMEPAGES

Personal webpages or homepages created early opportunities for self-expression across expansive, largely anonymous, digital networks. Personal webpages were textual forms with limited affordances for interactivity, which was restricted to replies to email links, signing guest books or posting on rant pages (Miller, 1995). Consequently they seem unpromising contexts for the realization of the dynamic, situated, generative forms of social interaction studied by Goffman and, therefore, unlikely to support self-formation and the generation of interaction orders. Recognizing the limits of interactivity in these online forms, Miller (1995, p. 5) interprets personal homepages as literary rather than dramatic forms, identifying self-presentational 'genres' based on content analysis of posts. Interestingly, this treats personal webpages as textual forms more akin to letters or messages in a bottle floated into anonymous digital networks than to face-to-face interaction. The types of content framing identified by Miller included 'Hi, this is us', consisting of displays of family or friendship group portraits, and 'I think this is cool', in which people presented themselves as cultural intermediaries through displays of 'cyber cool'. These forms of self-presentation sat alongside more instrumental posts, such as those looking for work or relationships or offering services. Similarly, Dominick's (1999) analysis of the content of homepages revealed them to display information about demographics, relatives, occupations, likes and dislikes and music preferences, alongside expressions of opinion, political attitudes and creative expressions.

Papacharissi (2002) interpreted self-presentation on personal homepages as offering opportunities for users to disseminate personal information to widespread, anonymous online audiences, and as a means of connecting with family, friends and colleagues. She picks up Goffman's (1959) discussion of information 'given' and 'given off', suggesting that 'A web page provides the ideal setting for this type of information game, allowing maximum control over the information disclosed' (Papacharissi, 2002, p. 644). In a reference to Goffman's emphasis on the richness of face-to-face, copresent interaction, Papacharissi argues that the 'absence of nonverbal elements may render communication less rich, but simultaneously allows individuals to be more inventive with self-presentation. There is greater control of expressions given off and thus less risk that identity manipulation may be exposed' (2002, p. 645). The idea that online environments provide greater control over information given compared to face-to-face encounters is a significant theme in early studies of self-presentation in online environments.

However, from Goffman's perspective, a critical aspect of self-presentation in social encounters is the participants' ability to check the consistency, appropriateness and validity of the claims people make about themselves using the cues available in the close proximity of face-to-face interaction. In the context of textual communication at a distance, control partly means a reduced chance that claims made and impressions created might be questioned, challenged, undermined, disrupted or contradicted by information 'given off' or through the careful observation and tests set by copresent others. According to Goffman, such tests create conditions of accountability that are crucial for self-formation and the collaborative nature and shared experience of copresent social interaction. This speaks to a contrast between the ethics of communication – in which face-to face interaction constrains overtly persuasive communication and the potential for deceit and creates the conditions for mutuality and collaborative social interaction – and an ethics of emotivism in which participants seek to control the impressions others form of them in order to persuade them of their good character (MacIntyre, 1981). The focus on control over the information given on personal webpages compared to face-to-face encounters suggests that early online environments supported an ethic of self-promotion and persuasion. In contrast, for Goffman, presenting the self in the best light is a cultural expectation that provides the grounding for trust in social relations, cooperation and shared experience rather than exclusively a strategy of persuasion. The textual context of personal webpages also allows participants to compose material before 'presenting' it online, as a form of edited self, in contrast to the dynamic construction of self-presentation in face-to-face encounters (Marwick, 2013; Ditchfield and Lunt, 2020). These contexts also suggest that early digital environments emphasized the individual expressive rather than the interactional aspects of self-presentation, such that mediated social interaction in these forms contributed to individualization at the expense of coordination and shared experience, thereby creating an interaction order based on control and persuasion rather than mutuality and the co-construction of social integration and relationships. Dominick (1999) recognizes that the limited forms of feedback on personal homepages constituted a culture of support or acclamation in contrast to the dynamic, co-constructed and accountable participation in face-to-face encounters. It becomes apparent that 'personal homepages, arguably the first multimedia online identity presentations, are highly managed and limited in collaborative scope; people tend to present themselves in fixed, singular, and self-conscious ways' (Marwick and boyd, 2011 p. 115). In early forms of digital self-presentation, content was king, as it was in mass communication, suggesting either a form of display to an audience or a means of reinforcing existing social relationships. The interactional forms of self-presentation are here more akin to those of an actor on stage or a presenter on broadcast media than to participation in the dynamic of face-to-face social interaction with its associated opportunities for self-formation and shared experience. However, although limited as forms of self-presentation, there were compensations that went beyond the reach of face-to-face social encounters, notably the availability of extended audiences for these performances of the self, the control over information given about the self, and the engagement in extended networks of connection beyond the limitations of the location of face-to-face encounters. These early studies point to an alternative imaginary of the social self in contrast to Goffman's interactionist view. The development of online multiplayer games led to a reconsideration of the concept of self being played out in digital environments, to which we now turn.

RECONCEPTUALIZING THE DIGITAL SELF

The anonymity of early digital environments allowed participants relative freedom from the typical constraints of face-to-face encounters in social contexts and from prejudicial appearance-based judgements of the kind Goffman identified in his study of stigma (1963a). Consequently, people were relatively free to express themselves and try out different online identities in an environment where they were not so exposed to prejudice and attitudes based on gender, ethnicity or physical appearance that required avoidance and management strategies in face-to-face interactions (Goffman, 1963a). This aspect of online social environments – their capacity to cut across borders and distinctions that play out in the offline world – led some to proclaim the potential freedoms of the internet as part of early cyber optimism (Donath, 2014). Another aspect of this idiom of self-expression was that these communication media were configured in terms of a relationship between clearly coded performers and audiences; even if the audiences were vast and anonymous, the roles were relatively fixed compared to the dynamic interplay of face-to-face interaction.

In addition to avoiding constraints and stigma, anonymity in digital environments enabled the playing out of imaginary or fantasy selves. The digital world was seen as an environment for play, fantasy and self-promotion, with the potential for a liberation of social identity. This way of thinking about the self was partly based on what appeared to be a radical separation between online spaces and everyday life. The subtle interplay between constraints and freedom that characterized Goffman's analysis of the dynamics of face-to-face social encounters was replaced by a view of online social life as a relatively free form of expression and experimentation. These apparent freedoms from constraint were identified as representing a radical shift in modern life with the combination of postmodern culture and new media technologies (Poster, 1995). A significant theme in the social theoretical literature of the time attempted to historicize the notion of the rational and autonomous self as characteristic of liberalism under modernity, which was now giving way to the postmodern condition. The alignment of digital media with postmodernity and the networked self (Papacharissi, 2010), understood as a decentred, free-floating form of social identity, had a seductive feel. However, it contrasted with the interactionist view that performed social identity, although not an essential part of individual identity, was meaningfully adapted to social contexts (Siles, 2017).

A related analysis of emerging forms of social identity can be found in Gergen's (1991) notion of the 'saturated self', which linked selfhood to an ever more complex technologically mediated public life not bound by the traditions of time, place and social community. Concrete examples included opportunities to choose screen names, gender and personality descriptions in the contexts of online multiplayer games, and websites in which avatars traversed virtual environments. However, this playful identity adoption with game characters was not seen in terms of its potential for creative self-construction, but as a potential source of feelings of power, self-efficacy or skill in gaming contexts in which the pleasure in establishing online relationships and the potential to explore neglected or new aspects of identity are more motivating than the potential to invent a fantasy self (Turkle, 1996). Ironically, Goffman is often cited in this literature as supporting the idea of self-formation as taking multiple, fragmented and disembodied forms. His view, however, being 'closer to symbolic interactionism', challenged this idea 'by noting that individuals do not transcend the physical body to elaborate many virtual selves but instead give multiple performances of the same self for different audiences' (Siles, 2017, p. 192).

Complementing these arguments for the postmodern or saturated self as realized in digital media contexts, evidence emerged suggesting that users adopted creative and experimental identities online as a way of playing with versions of themselves rather than radically new identities (see, for example, Chester and Bretherton, 2007). Users became adept at finding ways of expressing what they regarded as their authentic selves adapted to the idiom of game playing. Furthermore, content analysis of messages showed that participants often revealed their age, gender and location, fixing their online identities to features of their offline identities. In addition, the freedom-from-constraints argument was itself constrained by the emergence of online norms of self-presentation including 'friendliness and sense of humour . . . "fun-loving" presentations' (Chester and Bretherton, 2007, p. 226). These findings suggest that online identities could be interpreted as reflecting the symbolic interactionist view (including Goffman's) of the self which, while not adopting an essentialist account, contends that the self is meaningful in context and not free-floating, as had been suggested for a while. The findings also suggest that online identities reflect aspects of offline identities, which we will explore further when we look at self-presentation in social media. The adaptability of users in multiplayer game contexts also reflects Goffman's account of the social world as constituting different regions which we are used to traversing in our everyday lives and to which we adapt in both the offline and online worlds.

THE SELF IN SOCIAL MEDIA

In contrast to the textual forms of early web presence, with their limited scope for interaction and separation of offline and online worlds, Web 2.0 afforded 'multimedia features such as photos, videos, "gadgets", favourite music, personal biography, "friends" lists, and links to the blogger's social networking profiles' (Bullingham and Vasconcelos, 2013, p. 102), features which we now take up in relation to self-presentation, relationships and interaction orders in social media. As part of the public imagination of the internet, Web 2.0 was the label for a cluster of technological shifts that involved increased access to and opportunities for user-generated content and interactivity afforded by the interoperability of digital technologies in an emerging, widespread online participatory culture. As an urban myth, it is represented on Wikipedia thus: 'Web 2.0 refers to websites that emphasize user-generated content, ease of use, participatory culture and interoperability for end users. The term was coined by Darcy DiNucci in 1999 and later popularized by Tim O'Reilly and Dale Dougherty at the first Web 2.0 Conference in 2004.'

Nearly ten years later, Marwick (2013) reflected on the history of internet imaginaries which emerged following the erosion of early optimism arising from the bursting of the dotcom bubble, arguing that Web 2.0 created the conditions for the emergence of new, powerful Big Tech companies. Marwick links these developments to the increasing individualization of users as part of the spread of the political ideology of neoliberalism across the globe through the marketization of everyday life and the enrolling of the self in regimes of governmentality scaffolded by digital media enterprises.

Burgess et al. define social media as 'those digital platforms, services and apps built around the convergence of content sharing, public communication, and interpersonal connection' (2018, p. 1). In contrast to the limitations of earlier frameworks for self-presentation online, social media typically provide opportunities to publish a profile of personal information and to construct a list of contacts and a timeline or newsfeed through which a degree of interaction between participants is afforded by exchanging posts and responding to each other with tags, likes and comments (boyd and Ellison, 2007). Personal profile information is provided by completing a template, including name, date of birth and interests. Users can also structure the communication frameworks of their social media practice by, for example, forming different groups of contacts, communicating more privately with some of these contacts through an internal messaging system. In short, many of the features of Goffman's analysis of face-to-face social interaction were available in social media compared to previous technological platforms, providing opportunities for mediated interaction in a context that was shaped by powerful media corporations.

SELF-PRESENTATION IN SOCIAL MEDIA

Initially, the focus on information control identified in Papacharissi's (2002) study of personal webpages continued as a central theme in studies of self-presentations on social media, where the emphasis was on strategic impression management rather than the cut and thrust dynamics of face-to-face interaction identified by Goffman. In these studies, personal profile information and contact or friends' lists were understood as a resource for users to make inferences about each other based on their choice of contacts and what they post on their timelines. These sources provide significant personal information which can be used by individuals to create an impression of the self and also by participants to make inferences and check the claims made (Walther and Burgoon, 1992; Walther, 1996; Ellison et al., 2006; Walther et al., 2008). In this context, self-presentation as impression formation and management is regarded as a 'performance ... centred around public displays of social connections or friends, which are used to authenticate identity and introduce the self through the reflexive process of fluid association with social circles' (Chambers, 2013, p. 304). Walther et al. (2008) demonstrated that the information displayed in profiles can be searched by other users and used to judge or bring people to account, thus reproducing important elements of face-to-face interaction.

Developing this theme, Chambers (2013) notes that people use various methods to test the veracity of online claims, including checking alternative sources of information, examining other people's opinions about a person, and looking for evidence that is 'given off' to see if it supports what is explicitly communicated. All of these methods of checking out the claims made about the self in social interaction are observed in Goffman's (1959) studies of self-presentation in face-to-face encounters. However, online contexts enable participants to control the information that is displayed about them to a greater degree than in most face-to-face contexts. This is because, in the latter contexts, social interaction is a dynamic exchange in which the roles of performer and audience interchange as the interaction unfolds, various channels of communication are in play, and there are often several people present so we can watch people interacting with others. In short, interaction in social contexts combines opportunities for and constraints on self-presentation that are only partially replicated online. The relatively greater control over information displayed in online contexts allows participants to manage their online impressions by carefully selecting information for display, disguising any flaws, conforming to normative expectations and inflating positive personal qualities (Ellison et al., 2006). Also, boyd (2006) points out that a focus on impression management can constrain use of social media by, for example, constructing long lists to create a sense of popularity and making a careful choice of contacts to manage reputation by association.

In some online contexts – for example dating sites – a focus on impression management makes sense as a determinant of online self-presentation. Ellison et al.'s (2006) study of impression management strategies on dating sites highlights the tension between competing constraints in aiming to appeal to potential partners and providing authentic personal information as a foundation for a potential face-to-face encounter. The way that participants in such encounters scrutinize and check the claims people make about themselves is highly salient and creates a hyper-reflexive context (Gibbs et al., 2006). This contrasts somewhat with the routine accomplishment of and focus on collaboration in Goffman's account of impression formation which can result in a tendency to present an ideal self (Goffman, 1961b; Gibbs et al., 2006), motivated by an attempt to persuade others of one's good character by exaggerating traits or qualities in an attempt to ingratiate, or in conformity to a cultural norm to present one's best side (Goffman, 1959). In addition, in everyday contexts, the control of self-disclosure plays an important role in relationship development (Taylor and Altman, 1987) and reflects the interplay of secrets and the revelation of personal information in public settings (Goffman, 1959).

The focus on impression management in studies of social media was influenced by social psychological theories which were derived from but also a reduction of Goffman's (1959) analysis of self-presentation as dramaturgy. For example,

Schlenker, whose writing was influential on media studies of self-presentation on social media, developed an impression management theory in which 'people attempt to place themselves in beneficial circumstances through their selection of friends, mates, jobs and hobbies . . . and to influence those with whom they interact' (2012, p. 134). Impression management focuses on strategically managed social interaction as a social skill and as an essential part of human intelligence (Schlenker, 2012). Impression management also focuses on control, reflecting 'the seminal idea that people attempt to regulate and control, sometimes consciously and sometimes without awareness, the information they present to audiences, particularly information about themselves' (Schlenker and Weigold, 1992). In addition, Leary and Kowalski (1990) define impression management in terms of strategies of ingratiation, including 'false modesty' and praising others for being liked, presenting information about the self to draw attributions of competence, using power tactics such as threats or anger, or attempting to appear morally superior to others by presenting oneself as self-sacrificing or self-disciplined for the sake of a cause.

Impression management is certainly one strategy of self-presentation both in face-to-face encounters and online. However, it focuses on the information-game aspects of self-presentation and the provision of textual information on social media sites rather than on the interactional aspects of interplay on timelines including comments, likes and tags. Also, the focus on strategic interaction sets aside the interactional, cooperative and supportive aspects of social interaction. Interestingly, Goffman's own account of impression management in *The Presentation of Self in Everyday Life* was also concerned with group interaction and the role of teamwork in sustaining impressions, rather than being focused on information games.

Hogan (2010) questioned the application of Goffman's dramaturgical analysis of self-presentation to social media because of the lack of copresence and interaction therein. Hogan argued that status updates and posts on social media do not constitute social encounters in the sense intended by Goffman. He suggests that they are best considered as a form of curation and exhibition rather than dramatic self-presentation. First, the performer and the audience are not copresent; second, what is presented has a static form rather than developing through interaction; third, impression management studies tend to focus on relatively fixed, textual forms of self-disclosure on social media, such as profiles and contact lists, in contrast to Goffman's concern with the 'continual adjustment of self-presentation based on the presence of others' (Hogan, 2010, p. 378). However, even if participants in a social interaction exclusively listen, as in the theatre, their presence as spectators or witnesses is still critical to the performance and creation of the mise-en-scène. Also, notwithstanding Hogan's points about the lack of copresence and of interaction, there is a sense in which traces in digital media contexts can be a form of self-presentation that offers the audience various options through which to engage with posts on social media. A broader concern here is that, despite the variety of perspectives on the interaction order in Goffman's work, the focus has so far been almost exclusively on self-presentation and mediated impression management, at the expense of engaging with the different elements of his dramaturgy. In addition, there has been a lack of attention to his writings on ritual, face-work and strategic interaction and his broader commitment to interactionism, as a consequence of the focus on self-presentation.

THE INTERACTIONAL SELF ON SOCIAL MEDIA

Robinson (2007) also recognizes the focus on self-presentation and seeks to highlight the influence of Mead (1934) and symbolic interactionism (Blumer, 1992 [1969]) on Goffman's account of self-formation as a process achieved by reflexive agents through social interaction. Robinson offers a critical reconstruction of the potential for self-formation in the interactionist tradition in relation to digital environments, arguing that the elements of copresent, face-to-face interaction are unnecessary to self-formation in online social interaction. She also reminds us that Goffman does not offer a 'two-selves' theory that separates an internal sense of self from that performed through social interaction, and she argues against the idea of the postmodern or saturated self (Gergen, 1991). Instead she argues that there are continuities between the presentation of self in everyday life and in digital media contexts, and that Mead's conception of the self – including the 'I', the 'me' and the 'generalized other' – also plays out in socially mediated social interactions. Furthermore, Cooley's (1922) 'looking glass self' imagines how we appear to others, the judgements they might form of us and our feelings about these. Such experiences about the judgements people might make about us, including their perceptions and evaluations of our qualities, are an important part of our self-identity, complementing the identity we project through self-presentation.

Chambers (2013) and Robinson (2007) apply these ideas to the self as co-created through dynamic processes of social interaction in digital and social media, seeing them as constituting a 'digital other', a counterpart to Cooley's idea of our selves as reflected in the actions of others towards us and Mead's conception of the 'generalized other'. Robinson argues that reflexive self-consciousness only requires the presence of others who can see us or try to influence us to create a dynamic process of self-formation. For example, the perception of the audience for a social media post ('who is watching me?') is a source of social comparison in which people consider how the audience might expect them to behave, which can be generalized in the anticipated judgement of the imagined audience in digital or social media. In addition, there are also examples of other features of the interaction order in play in social media. For example, Uski and Lampinen (2014) identify sharing as a form of cooperative practice in self-presentation on Facebook and Last.FM. Another feature of the accountability of conduct in social interaction that Goffman identified in face-to-face interaction is the constraint on 'control' provided by others being able to observe and monitor our actions and potentially bring them to account. Uski and Lampinen recognize that liking, commentary and other forms of feedback are forms of social interaction outside individual participants' control that provide constraints on self-presentation.

Bullingham and Vasconcelos (2013) also set the study of online self-presentation in the broader conceptualization of Goffman's dramaturgy, distinguishing between heightened self-consciousness in the frontstage compared to immersive engagement backstage. Performance in the frontstage involves the risk of loss of face and requires the management of information 'given' and 'given off'. Bullingham and Vasconcelos suggest that, as Goffman (1959) argued on many occasions, performers, audiences and teams seek to display selective aspects of their backstage identity as a kind of edited self (see also Marwick, 2013). Consequently, even when participants play with identity forms, these are often symbols of or extrapolations from their character, such that a mask is not simply hiding an identity but rather emphasizing specific aspects of that identity. The social media context encompasses, sometimes blurring, aspects of social frontstages, with an emphasis on roles and persuasion and the more relaxed modes of interaction in the backstages of social life.

SOCIAL MEDIA AND EVERYDAY LIFE

Studies of self-presentation in social media developed as part of the increasing recognition of the integration of social media and everyday life practices, relationships and communities. In contrast to earlier forms of digital communication, social media are grounded in everyday life partly because of the variety of social relationships they encompass, including relations with family, friends and online acquaintances, creating a mixture of strong and weak social ties (boyd, 2006). Whereas everyday life is played out across various locations and contexts with their associated social relationships, social media blurs these distinctions in a collapsed context (Marwick and boyd, 2011). While the regions and contexts of everyday life bring people together in shared social relationships among family, friends, classmates or work companions, in social media participants in different social relations can all observe our posts. For example, Ellison et al.'s (2006) informants use Facebook to keep in touch with old friends, intensify current friendships and reinforce local friendship groups or geographically close relationships.

Challenging the idea that the internet is reducing the importance of locale and existing relationship networks, Blackwell et al. (2015) draw on Baym's (2010) analysis of personal connections in the internet age to examine how location-finding apps can be used to arrange meetings or hook-ups with new people so that 'today's internet layers physical and online spaces' (Blackwell et al., 2015, p. 1118). Similarly, Miller shows how Trinidadians use Facebook as a social 'buffer' for people who may be 'potential friends' without requiring 'awkward face-to-face interaction' (2011, p. 165). Chen and Lunt (2021) demonstrate how the affordances of WeChat allow for multiple groups and control over individual posts that sustains multiple interaction orders within the same platform.

Social media is integrated within everyday life through appropriation by friendship groups and local cultures. For example, Livingstone (2008), working with young people online, described how some of her informants wrote joke profiles that did not match their actual circumstances. They might say they were in a relationship or married to someone when they were not. Livingstone suggests that these are strategies for building peer groups beyond the online space, arguing that such tales are more about displaying the self (as fun and lively) and play than a desire to deceive. Livingstone (2008, p. 396) also proposes that teenagers may adopt the 'online realm' because it is 'their' space, visible to their peer group more than their parents and teachers, and represents an exciting yet relatively safe place in which to take risks as part of a developing sense of personal identity (see Boyd, 2014).

Tuğçe Ozansoy Çadırcı and Ayşegül Sağkaya Güngör (2019) examined the role of selfies in impression management on social networks, following the work of van Dijck (2013) on conscious self-promotion and Hogan's (2010) analysis of the curation of the online self in the context of social media as a dynamic medium for self-expression (Mendelson and Papacharissi, 2010). They analysed self-formation in social media as an example of an 'extended self' played out in the digital world through self-presentation (Goffman, 1959). Selfies are an extension of the body that affords an extended self-image in a hybrid of actual and ideal forms that 'facilitate self-enhancement and self-presentation more acceptably' (Ozansoy Çadırcı and Sağkaya Güngör,

2019, p. 269). Ozansoy Çadırcı and Sağkaya Güngör argue that selfies are pure frontstages with no backstage, affording a particular focus on Goffman's (1959) analysis of the material aspects of self-presentation as a front that combined appearance and manner. In visual self-presentation, a conscious effort is made on appearance rather than manner, through make-up, clothing and artefacts. The self, therefore, appears in a re-materialized form as a carefully curated photograph (Hogan, 2010). Sylvester (2019) explored Goffman's (1959) account of self-presentation in the context of selfies produced by contemporary feminist artists who challenge gendered representations of the body through the creative representation of their own bodies, extending the idea of portraiture to self-presentation, as explored in Goffman's (1979) *Gender Advertisements*. Sylvester shows 'how Instagram as a platform provides a stage for identity work that offers an opportunity to explore visual self-branding, the potential of narrative construction of identity via selfies and the effect of social media on identity construction' (2019, p. 61).

These different examples of self-presentation in a variety of social arrangements contrast with the idea of social media as a separate reality; they continue the tradition of symbolic interactionist accounts of the self in which 'Sociology has long conceptualised persons as occupying multiple positions in organised sets of social relationships, and as playing out the diverse roles associated with those multiple positions' (Stryker and Burke, 2000, p. 290).

ONLINE RITUAL, FACE AND FACE-WORK

While the complications of self-presentation and impression management have been a significant focus of attention in the study of social media, Goffman's analysis of social interaction as ritual, including his analysis of face-work and civility, has attracted less interest. Recognizing this trend, Ivana (2014, 2016) applied ideas from Goffman's (1967) analysis of face-work to social relations played out on Facebook. Ivana (2016) suggests that, in contrast to impression management, understood as projecting or displaying an established social identity (real or imaginary) online, face-work and civility are processes of self-formation accomplished through social interaction, and that social media platforms such as Facebook afford a relational approach to supporting and recognizing face or reputation.

Ivana (2016) identifies posts on timelines using tagging, likes and comments as a form of recognition and respect towards others and as lines or themes of self-expression adopted in Facebook posts. There is a degree of common courtesy involved in using these responses on Facebook, which are equivalent to the mundane ritual forms of polite greetings, supportive nods and verbal encouragements that Goffman (1955, 1967) identified in face-to-face social encounters. Alongside these forms of social support that operate by recognizing and praising an individual in support of their face, Ivana (2016) also follows Goffman (1967) in recognizing threats to face that potentially decrease users' confidence and self-worth. In his studies on face-work, Goffman (1955, 1967) acknowledged the duality of the Chinese concept of face in terms of its recognition of achievement and of standing in the community. Face as *mianzi*, feeling good about one's achievements as acknowledged by others, can increase or decrease according to the level of recognition received from others. More likes and comments in response to achievement claims on Facebook or WeChat can increase self-esteem (Chen and Lunt, 2021). In contrast, *lian*, or the respect afforded to another based on being a respected community member, operates more like social exclusion because it is granted as a right to all but can be removed if community members feel a person is not worthy of recognition. On social media, most feedback appears to be achievement-oriented, and self-esteem is a consciousness of recognition by others that can wax and wane. In other words, it is a form of reflexive self-monitoring that depends on ritual forms of recognition from one's online community. Interestingly, on social media, individuals tend to develop an ethic of care of the self by granting themselves *mianzi* through self-attribution, complementing recognition granted by others (Chen and Lunt, 2021).

Lim and Basynet (2016) distinguish between the face oriented towards self and towards others and the mutual co-construction of face. They recognize the Chinese cultural distinction between *mianzi* and *lian*, and that deference, conviviality and recognition are linked to feelings of dignity, pride and shame that are visible online across various Asian cultures on Twitter, Facebook and Instagram. They also emphasize that the Chinese concept of face is not a claim that individuals make for themselves but is given or taken away through social interactions in social relationships (*guanxi*). As in Ivana's (2016) study, the processes of gaining or giving face are recognized in liking, sharing, commenting, favouriting and retweeting, all affordances for self-work and civility that reflect Goffman's analysis of mundane, ritual forms of recognition and deference.

Goffman's (1967) work on deference and demeanour goes beyond recognition of individuals' social standing to include the idea that through such interactions participants construct a culture of civility and care of the self (Lim and Basynet, 2016; Chen and Lunt, 2021). Mulyana and Qomariana (2023) examined face-maintaining rituals and strategies on YouTube. They emphasize the multilingual context of Indonesia in which there is a tradition of paying attention to those we interact with along the lines of Goffman's (1967) analysis of deference and demeanour. Goffman adapted ideas from Durkheim's (1995 [1912]) sociology of religion, which used the anthropological record of rituals governing who has access to the sacred totem that symbolizes the group and their comportment towards and behaviour in its presence. Adopting these ideas, Mulyana and Qomariana (2023) identify presentation rituals and avoidance rituals on YouTube as forms of deference and the maintenance of social distance among participants. Interestingly, the dominant form of ritual is presentation rituals, which are used to express face and to save others' faces with less emphasis on the constitution of a culture of civility (Geuss, 2001). We will return to these questions in Chapter 5, concerning social media as a cultural environment and debates about the power of Big Tech and the opportunities for participants to constitute the culture they inhabit, which was a critical question in Goffman's analysis of social interaction as constitutive practice (Rawls, 2011, 2012, 2022).

COPRESENCE

Goffman based his empirical research on the observation and analysis of copresent, face-to-face interaction in everyday social encounters. He regarded copresence as a necessary condition for nuanced, dynamic social interactions which, in turn, create the conditions for the performance of self-presentation, ritual forms of the recognition of social standing, playful engagements, strategies for managing institutional constraints on agency, ways of coping with prejudice, and the social organization of experience. In contrast, mediation implies distance in space and time between participants, thereby potentially compromising the capacity of social interaction to form interaction orders and to realize the associated social processes. Goffman did acknowledge that media could find ways to partially compensate for the limitations of mediated social interaction compared to face-to-face interaction and to possibly augment mediated social interaction. However, overall, he was sceptical about this. Consequently, the study of mediated copresence is a crucial part of the argument about mediated interaction, which we explore in this section through examples from the study of mediated copresence, virtual social presence, being there together (Schröder, 2010) and virtual copresence (Madianou, 2016).

Although Goffman used a variety of examples of copresence throughout his work, he did not explicitly define the concept and it remained, to a degree, a taken-for-granted assumption of his analysis of situated social encounters. He identified various elements of copresence, such as bodily proximity, being together at the same time and place, coordinating actions and reactions, sharing experiences, and being in a rich environment with various channels of communication, including verbal, visual and non-verbal cues. Experientially, Goffman drew on Schutz's (1967) analysis of the phenomenology of the social world to distinguish the different orientations that individuals have towards one another in social encounters. The development of digital media technologies increasingly affords the experience of connection, immersion, coordination, sharing and a sense of 'being there' (Schroeder, 2010), potentially changing the argument about the qualities of mediated interaction compared to face-to-face encounters.

Researchers who studied early mobile communications were impressed by how it afforded contact with significant others and detached telephone communication from place (Robinson, 2007; Ling, 2008). They argued that this advanced connectivity amounted to copresence, with individuals able to sustain social relations as nodes in networks of connection rather than being fixed by place. One response was to distinguish between presence and copresence, along with a proliferation of terms such as telepresence, virtual presence and mediated presence (Lee, 2004). Another impetus came from virtual reality systems, a salient development driven by claims about reproducing 'being there' (Schroeder, 2010). In this section, I will review examples from the literature that connects Goffman's analysis of social interaction to mediated copresence (Licoppe, 2004), virtuality (Schroeder, 2010) and mediated ambient copresence (Madianou, 2016).

Licoppe (2004) explored presence in the context of mobile communications using calls and text messaging in the days before smartphones. He argued that social relationships have historically exploited the available communication technologies and therefore inevitably incorporated the affordances of mobile communications in the organization of social encounters and social relationships. Significantly, Licoppe regarded mobile phone encounters as moments in a life lived as a 'single seamless web', 'a continuous pattern of mediated interactions that combine into a connected relationship' (2004, p. 136). He also distinguished between long calls on mobiles that create a space for the performance of a conversation and shorter 'message' calls that punctuate everyday life. These ideas speak to mediated social encounters and sociality as a narrative constructed through connections that create meaning in the flows of everyday life.

While Goffman focused on interaction and, therefore, copresence as part of social practice, much of the work on the experience of others in mediated connection and virtuality has focused on the perceptual aspects of simulated environments and, if other agents are involved, on the social psychological tradition of studying the effects of the presence of others on individuals. Consequently, there has been a much greater focus on presence than on copresence in virtual reality studies. To counter this, Schultze and Brooks (2019) sought to develop an interactional account of virtual social presence in place of a common approach in information systems that regards presence as the awareness of those present and interaction as a feature of the scene. Copresence, according to this view, is seen as exhausted by an awareness of the inner states communicated by others and the coordination of movements and positioning of the body in space. The disclosure of psychological states through non-verbal communication interested Goffman and was a crucial part of his account of information given and given off in social interaction. However, he had more to say about copresence and, by extension, potentially more to offer the study of virtual copresence, as Schultze and Brooks suggest, following the lead of Baym (2015) and Walter and Burgoon (1992), by asking the Goffmanian question: 'How is social presence accomplished in virtual environments?' (Schultze and Brooks, 2019, p. 708).

In an observational study of Second Life focusing on Goffman's (1963b) concepts of involvement and involvement obligation from *Behavior in Public Places*, Schultze and Brooks (2019) sought an understanding of social presence as a cooperative social accomplishment that plays a constitutive role in organizing virtual experience as 'real'. In Goffman's work (1963b, p. 36), involvement combined bodily states and orientations, attention and feelings, leading to dispositions to act and co-construct experiences through interaction. The multidimensional features of face-to-face interaction afforded a sense of real involvement for participants in a social encounter: 'Something in which the individual can become unselfconsciously engrossed is something that can become real to him' (Goffman, 1961b, p. 80).

In addition to the analysis of the organization of behaviour in public places, Goffman's (1974) analysis of the organization of experience drew on two other ideas from Schutz's (1967) phenomenology: the recognition of various modes of orientation towards others in social interaction and the idea of the social world as presenting multiple realities. The experience of others in social situations involves coordination, social influence, recognition, mutual constitution of social practices and acknowledgement of social relations that are emergent and not reducible to individual experience. These aspects of sociality are potentially realizable through digital media as well as face-to-face social interaction and create a challenge to virtual or augmented reality that seeks to include social interaction. The potential links between Goffman's work and media phenomenology will be explored further in Chapter 5.

An example of social interaction as coordinated activity that affirms social relationships in everyday life is the use of digital and social media in contexts of distant family life resulting from migration or travel abroad for work or education (Madianou and Miller, 2012; Chen and Lunt, 2021). Digital and social media have a variety of affordances that enable people to sustain family life, including providing opportunities for shared experience or being together (Schroeder, 2010). In their everyday lives, families spend time together on mundane activities such as meals, watching television, going out to eat, chatting, etc. For young adults and their parents, one of the difficulties of separation from the family home is missing such everyday rituals of family life. Digital media enable a version of hanging out together, which Madianou (2016) calls 'ambient copresence', in which people contact each other through social media such as Skype, WhatsApp or WeChat to share routine time as they might at home. Madianou gives the example of being in contact while cooking, which involves sporadic chatting and gives a sense of living together even while being physically apart.

These examples illustrate the potential of mediated shared experiences and social practices and suggest other modes of being with others beyond coordinating or synchronizing activities and parallel practices, including broader forms of social relations that recognize and constitute mutual activities in we-relations, offering a potentially fruitful route into the study of the role of digital media in the organization of experience (Goffman, 1974). In addition, mundane forms of virtual reality might be understood from the perspective of transitions between multiple realities along the lines of Goffman's frame analysis, developed using Schutz's conception of multiple realities.

Digital media also expand the capacity for forms of conversational copresence (Licoppe, 2004) by reducing the cost of talking compared to telephone contact, affording a mix of audio and video messaging so that parents and children living at a distance can have periodic conversations to update each other on what is happening in their lives and express concerns or share achievements. These studies have added nuance to the idea of perpetual contact (Katz and Aakhus, 2002), demonstrating the use of various technologies or combinations of technologies in different modes of sociability to sustain family life and relations at a distance. Madianou and Miller (2012) have shown that while these expanded opportunities for contact, information sharing and copresence are welcome they can also involve tensions. Attempts to parent, whether through encouragement or discipline, are difficult to sustain through these modes of parenting at a distance.

MEDIATED SOCIAL INTERACTION: PARTICIPATION FRAMEWORKS

In his essay on 'footing' in *Forms of Talk*, Goffman (1981) analysed how social encounters were organized as communication frameworks in which participants in the production and reception of utterances adopted different communication roles. In social interactions, communication frameworks influence participants' roles in interaction, although the roles adopted and the relationships between participants can change during a social encounter: 'A change in footing implies a change in alignment we take up to ourselves and the others present as expressed in the way we manage the production or reception of an utterance' (Goffman, 1981, p. 128).

In addition to capturing the dynamics of social interaction, Goffman was also motivated to challenge the established linguistic categories of speaker/hearer from a pragmatic perspective. In social encounters, people typically have different rights to speak as ratified or unratified participants, which Goffman took as an example of the decomposition of the roles of speaker and hearer into various roles in the production and reception of communication. Production roles include that of the animator, who provides the voice for the communication but who may be someone other than the author who wrote the words. In contrast, the principal is the person who authorizes or is responsible for the words spoken. Traditionally, the speaker does all these things, but these roles might be disaggregated in social contexts. In the theatre, for example, the playwright is the author, the actor is the animator, and the director is the principal. The hearer is similarly deconstructed as either the focus of the communication or an addressee, whereas other participants can be peripheral and unaddressed, although they may hear what is going on as witnesses or spectators. They can act as innocent overhearers or eavesdrop on the conversation. Participation frameworks also instantiate typical states of talk. In some formal or ceremonial contexts there is a dominant mode in terms of who has the right to speak and to play different communication roles. In less formal contexts there can be byplay in which, for example, unaddressed participants are addressed, and participants might go off message to discuss something not in focus in the interaction as a form of 'crossplay'. Alternatively, those who do not have the right to speak in the focal conversation can nevertheless engage in discussion of what is unfolding as a form of side play (Goffman, 1981).

Livingstone and Lunt (1994) applied Goffman's analysis of 'footing' to the analysis of social interactions in television talk shows. The shows were constructed partly by assigning different communication roles to the host, guests and studio audience. More recently, these ideas have been applied to digitally and socially mediated interaction. Hutchby (2014) argues that the interactional affordances of digital media create a proliferation of mediated language use. Hutchby paired elements of Goffman's (1981) analysis of the participation framework with an analysis of the affordances of digital communication technologies (Hutchby, 2001). The multimodality of language in digitally mediated social interaction (Kress, 2010) affords the interpolation of talk, non-verbal communication, texts and images, which are organized as communication frameworks. The task is to understand how participants 'organise and structure their participation in these multimodal and affordance-laden environments' (Hutchby, 2014, p. 87). Hutchby also reminds us of the long history of the mediation of language through writing, drawing, ceremony and print as part of our social and cultural history. Technologies of interaction also have a history, for example in the development of the microphone and the television camera (Scannell, 1996, 2014), which 'had particular communicative affordances that allowed the voice of the announcer, or the singer, the newsreader, comedian or actor, to be heard as if addressed intimately to the listener as a copresent individual' (Hutchby, 2014, p. 87). The papers in a journal special issue edited by Hutchby seek to 'demonstrate, in a whole range of ways, the continuing vitality of these concepts in facilitating our understanding of language-in-interaction even as the forms of technological mediation in society multiply and diversify' (2014, p. 87).

Ayaß (2014) discusses Goffman's (1963b) idea of 'territories of the self in public space' in which individuals seek to recuse themselves from obligations using a variety of 'involvement shields' that create a sense of their attention being focused elsewhere, for example by reading a book or newspaper. Ayaß demonstrates how the material form of digital communication technologies has enabled them to be used as 'involvement shields' that exempt users from the obligation to interact and place the burden on other participants to interrupt them, thereby violating the rule of civil inattention in public life (Geuss, 2001; Ayaß, 2014). This complicates the distinction between copresent and distant, suggesting that hybrid forms of public and private spaces often characterize public life.

Other papers in the special issue edited by Hutchby demonstrate that the spread and diversification of forms of digitally mediated participation frameworks are becoming integral to social participation in everyday life. Different Web 2.0 formats are identified, mapping the role of participants as producers through blogging and vlogging (Frobenius, 2014), posting videos or commenting on YouTube (Boyd, 2014), social networking (Eisenlauer, 2014) and engaging with online news publications. As Hutchby (2014) suggests, these are not mere adoptions of Goffman's concept of participation framework, although they demonstrate its continuing relevance, but demonstrate how the digital context extends Goffman's ideas about participation frameworks into new forms of digitally mediated social interaction. The roles of animator, author and principal on the production side, and forms of reception by ratified and non-ratified participants, are now played out with the wider 'perceptual range' provided by digital media (Hutchby, 2014, p. 89). Hutchby suggests that discussion fora and social media have sufficient elements of organization afforded by network providers and participants to lead to the re-emergence of conventional forms of address and civility, albeit in a modulated, often more playful or ironic form, as community formats (Baym, 2010).

Graham and Hardaker (2017) applied aspects of Goffman's (1981) analysis of participation frameworks to study communicative roles in digital media contexts where interactional affordances are extended to large-scale, dispersed participation frameworks beyond copresence. For example, 'lurkers' take the form of ratified participants who operate as bystanders. In digitally mediated interactions, we can be an overseer or overhearer, ratified or not, participant or lurker (Graham and Hardaker, 2017). There is scope to extend the study of social media through the lens of 'footing' as a way of exploring liking, tagging and commenting as ritual forms of recognition and as the constitution of a civil substrate in social media.

CONCLUSION

The proliferation of digital and mobile media and their integration into everyday life creates an environment where interpersonal communication and social relationships, two core features of the interaction order, are routinely mediated as part of the proliferation of language and interaction in the digital environment (Hutchby, 2014). Digital interpersonal connection (Katz and Aakhus, 2002) and engagement in public life (Burgess and Baym, 2020) have become standard

features of everyday life in a media environment of hyperconnectivity (Brubaker, 2020). Digital media technologies
are integrated into everyday life, extending the scope of
interpersonal and public communication, affording new ways
of organizing everyday life and social relationships.

These changes raise the possibility of mediating social
interaction with implications for Goffman's analysis of the
interaction order and its relation to social life. Here, I focus
on one of the questions raised by changes in the culture of
everyday life for understanding the affordances for social
interaction as a mediator of action and sociality (Hutchby,
2014). Language use and social interaction are proliferat-
ing in the digital age and they correlate with and shape the
design and use of digital media in different ways to previous communication technologies such as writing, letters,
radio and television (Hutchby, 2014). In addition, social relations in the family at a distance are infused with multiple
forms of digital media as polymedia (Madianou and Miller,
2012), while textual, visual and vocal forms of communication are remediated through messaging and video posts, with
a similar proliferation of ways people can connect and group
together. Goffman's ideas have been appropriated across the
divide of linear and digital media and encompass early, text-
based forms of digital media, although personal webpages
seem to be poor relations of Goffman's ideal of copresent,
face-to-face interaction.

Goffman's concepts of self-presentation information
games, 'given' and 'given off', were liberally used to analyse
mediated self-presentation in these new media forms. As
researchers at the time suggested (Miller, 1995), elements
of Goffman's analysis were visible in these early new media
environments, but, as Hogan (2010) argued, they lacked the
interactional dynamic that was so crucial to Goffman's conception of social interaction. While early, text-based forms of

digital media appeared to grant control over self-presentation (Papacharissi, 2002), social media introduced new elements in mediated practices of everyday life: instead of anonymity, there is identity; instead of a brave new world of possibility, there is integration with everyday life; instead of imagination and escape, there is the mediatization of everyday life.

Initially, researchers focused on impression management because social media included expanded information about users that can be inferred from their profiles, contact lists and timelines – the digital media equivalent of information 'given off', and just as open to feigning and fabrication as face-to-face interaction. It was possible to broadcast the self and to gain control over non-intentional dimensions of communication in a context that was less accountable to fellow interactants than that of face-to-face encounters, in line with Goffman's scepticism about mediated social interaction.

The engagement with self-presentation and control that was the focus of early studies of digitally mediated interaction was complemented by the realization that other aspects of Goffman's interaction order, such as ritual forms of civility in face-work, extended forms of copresence, and the playing out of communication roles in online contexts, are part of mediated social interaction and a potential area of development in our understanding of interactivity in an integrated digital media culture. These different studies suggest that the affordances of digital media have changed the argument about the contrast between face-to-face and mediated social interaction. The dichotomy between these two, and its instantiation in the distinction between interpersonal and mediated communication, presents a problematic contrast. What emerges is an account of different modalities of the mediation of social interaction in which elements of the rich environment of face-to-face encounters are made available through digital media. The distinction between interpersonal and mediated communication implies that the sociological impacts of social interaction such as self-formation, the formation of publics, and the relation between forms of order in social systems and everyday life may be extended to digitally mediated social interaction, which is the topic of the next chapter.

4

INTERACTIONISM AND
MEDIA SOCIOLOGY

INTRODUCTION

In Chapter 3, I explored the potential for mediated social interaction to afford elements of Goffman's analysis of the interaction order. In this chapter, I will review examples of how media scholars have attempted to link Goffman's interactionism with accounts of the role of media in society. While Goffman's observations and analyses of interactional forms are well developed in his work, the relation between the interaction order and societal processes and structures are less clearly articulated. As discussed in Chapter 1, Goffman's work does not fit within a single tradition of sociological research and is eclectic in its engagements. Although he made many suggestions about links, these were to various theories and approaches to sociology. The same problem faces media researchers who wish to relate analysis of the mediated interaction order to broader societal processes. This chapter explores the links between mediated ritual

interactions and social solidarity (Ling, 2008); the relation of
media culture to transformations of the family, gender relations and political culture (Meyrowitz, 1985); media framing
and hegemony (Benford and Snow, 2000); the social implications of broadcast talk (Scannell, 1991; Livingstone and
Lunt, 1994); the role of digital media in the formation of the
public (Marwick and boyd, 2011; Burgess and Baym, 2020);
the relationship between public and private in political culture (Thompson, 2018); and self-formation through digital
media (Brubaker, 2020).

CEREMONY, RITUAL AND INTERACTION RITUAL CHAINS

Mobile communication makes us personally contactable
wherever we might be, unlike the fixed location of landline
phones, which Goffman regarded as a limited form of communication. Ling (2008) sees mobility as a means to sustain
social relationships at a distance and to form social solidarity,
against the grain of influential arguments that modern life,
due to processes of individualization (Kraut et al., 1998; Nie,
2001), detaches people from communities and social relations with a consequent loss of social capital (Putnam, 2020).
In contrast, Ling argues that mobile ritual interactions can
potentially reinforce and strengthen social ties (Granovetter,
1973) with family members, friends and colleagues, and that
links between chains of mobile interactions constitute a form
of social solidarity that contributes to social cohesion in a
network society.

Drawing on Goffman's (1967) analysis of mundane social
interactions as rituals, Ling argues, with illustrations from
his studies of mobile phone use, that the kind of face-work,
deference and demeanour observed by Goffman (1967)
takes place routinely in mobile phone exchanges between

individuals with close social ties. Ling views such encounters as micro-ceremonies, in which individuals focus on each other in a shared structure of feeling to reaffirm their social ties. This process reflects Durkheim's understanding of social solidarity resulting from ceremonies, which draw clan members together through a shared experience of collective effervescence that reinforces collective commitment and identification with the totem as the symbol of the clan or society. Significantly, Ling argues that such experiences are linked together to form interactional ritual chains (Collins, 2004), thereby contributing to social cohesion.

Ling acknowledges Goffman's insight into mundane, everyday forms of ritual interaction, but argues that Goffman does not explain how such rituals involve the collective effervescence that symbolically charges the totem. He argues that Goffman was working at the individual level rather than the collective, examining 'how the individual rather than the totem is symbolically charged through social interaction' (2008, p. 91). In fact, Ling suggests that 'Goffman's interpretation of Durkheim does not carry with it the notion of the totem. Indeed, there is no mention of the word in his oeuvre' (p. 65).

Goffman's appropriation of Durkheim can be read not as offering a diminished form of ceremony but rather as an analysis of face-work and civility realized through ritual interactions that contribute to social solidarity. Goffman was influenced by Durkheim's duality of social identity (*homo duplex*), which contrasted the strategic, utility-maximizing aspects of social identity with that part of our social selves that reflects our embedding in social life and relationships as 'one apportionment of the collective *mana*', such that 'rites performed to representations of the social collective will sometimes be performed to the individual himself' (Goffman, 1967, p. 47). In this reading, greeting someone or complimenting them is not to be understood as a strategic action, even if on some occasions it can be, but rather as a moment of recognition of the common humanity shared by participants, symbolizing a society based on human rights and participation in a democratic culture (Jacobsen, 2010). Rather than thinking of such occasions as micro-ceremonies in which people experience shared emotions that reinforce social norms and cultural values, Goffman referenced Durkheim's analysis of the positive and negative rites that govern access to and behaviour in the presence of the totem in premodern religion. Goffman's account of the link between everyday ritual forms and social cohesion did not propose the aggregation of chain relations between individuals, but dispersed episodes of organic social solidarity that repeatedly symbolized and reflected commitments to human rights.

Durkheim (1995 [1912]) distinguished between mechanical and organic forms of social solidarity, and the example of the recognition of common humanity in mundane ritual forms of social interaction is a form of organic solidarity. Mechanical solidarity is reinforced through ceremony as a shared experience and rehearsal of the social norms and cultural values symbolizing the clan. Organic solidarity, in contrast, recognizes that in complex, pluralistic societies the potential for consensus is limited, and that social solidarity is more likely to be found in mutual recognition between individuals. Through care and maintaining appropriate distance by way of civil inattention, individuals treat each other as sacred carriers of human rights. Although Goffman did not explicitly use the term 'totem', there are passages where it is evident that he was referring to this aspect of Durkheim's account of the sociology of religion: 'Many gods have been done away with, but the individual himself stubbornly remains as a deity of considerable importance. He walks with some dignity and is the recipient of many little offerings. He is jealous of the worship due to him, yet, approached in the right spirit, he is ready to forgive those who may have offended him' (Goffman, 1967, p. 94). The development of social media in a network society constitutes digital hyper-connection (Brubaker, 2020), the sheer scale of which, along with its infiltration into every aspect of social and cultural life, provides a mechanism for the expansion of recognition as a form of social solidarity.

NO SENSE OF PLACE

Meyrowitz's *No Sense of Place* (1985), a classic in the field, combines elements of Goffman's interactionism and McLuhan's medium theory to analyse the impact of media culture on social behaviour. From Goffman, Meyrowitz took insights into the importance of social interaction for social life, the conception of the social world structured as sepa-rate regions, and the distinction between private and public spaces exemplified by Goffman's (1959) distinction between frontstage and backstage. From McLuhan (1964), Meyrowitz took the idea that media connect people to places and events that are outside of their local spheres of social exist-ence, thereby creating a global village that radically extends human perception and experience, transcending the limits of face-to-face perception and blurring the division of social life into local and distant regions. Visions of other lives and cultures penetrate the walls of the family home, blurring the boundary between the private world of the home and the public world made visible by media culture, granting access to visions of other cultures and ways of living. From the per-spective of media audiences, television acts like a portal to an expanded global culture, vastly extending the range of perception, experience and access to sources of information and variations in culture. For those who appear on television, it makes aspects of what previously might have been their private lives visible. Those exposed to these trends need to create a deep backstage to protect their privacy.

Meyrowitz examined the broader impacts of exposure to global media culture and the increasing visibility of the private lives of those who appear on television. He argued that these changes transformed social interaction, relationships and experience and blurred the distinction between public and private. Meyrowitz illustrated these changes through the blurring of the distinction between masculinity and femininity, affecting the interactions and relations between genders in the direction of greater equality, and the emergence of more liberal family relationships in which parents and children interact on an equal basis, exemplifying broader reductions in social hierarchy and deference in political culture.

No doubt the media played its part in increasing the visibility of political actors, and access to information on a global scale brought people into contact with various cultures and social practices. However, changes in gender relations and identity, the liberalization of relations between parents and children, and reduced deference towards those in authority were strongly influenced by the life politics movements of the 1960s and 1970s (Gitlin, 1987) and associated social changes such as the democratization of the family (Giddens, 1991a), while the blurring of gender identities reflected the application of ideas from the feminist movement to everyday life (Boltanski and Chiapello, 2006). Meyrowitz's interpretation of the liberalization of political culture in 1985 is also somewhat surprising in the context of the first Reagan administration, which was part of the conservative turn in political culture with its reassertion of many of the distinctions that appeared to have been blurred by media culture. Subsequent history is not unambiguously associated with more liberal gender representations and relations, the democratization of the family and a more open political culture. Political culture has since been transformed by identity politics, populism, the professionalism of promotional culture and the increasingly performative basis of self-presentation. The impacts discussed by Meyrowitz of the blurring of boundaries, extended engagement with people and events across the globe and the increased publicity of previously secret or private information have been radically exacerbated by digital and social media. These points illustrate the complexities of linking Goffman's work on social interaction with accounts of social transformation and the challenges of explaining social change from a media perspective.

THE MEDIA AND MODERNITY

Thompson (1995) suggested that the role of communication media in modernization had been understated by classic social theorists who focused on mapping the contours of transformation in the economic and political spheres. He argued that the importance of economic and political power in a global context is complemented by the importance of symbolic power (Bourdieu, 1991). Thompson drew on insights from Bourdieu (1991) to argue that symbolic power and its associated institutions should be added to economic and political power in accounts of modernization: 'What Bourdieu was pointing to here is that, in addition to money, property, and social connections, people in the strategic pursuit of their ends exploit cultural distinction and knowledge, interactional style, information, and reputation' (Clegg and Haugaard, 2009, p. 151).

The concept of symbolic power includes aspects of Goffman's analysis of the interaction order in the form of interaction style, information and reputation. Thompson illustrates the operation of symbolic power through the relation between self-formation and social interaction in a changing media environment. He argued that self-formation is increasingly interwoven with mediated symbolic forms: 'with the development of modern societies, the process of self-formation becomes more reflexive and open-ended, in the sense that individuals fall back increasingly on their resources to construct a coherent identity for themselves' (Thompson, 1995, p. 207). In the context of mass communication, Thompson sees the media as providing 'symbolic materials, greatly expanding the range of options available to individuals and loosening, without destroying, the connection between self-formation and shared locale' (p. 207). However, when compared with face-to-face communication, mass media is 'mediated quasi interaction' (Thompson, 1995), constructed to create a sense of intimacy (Scannell, 1991), although it is an asymmetric, non-dialogic, one-to-many form of communication. Mass communication exhilarates while creating an illusion of mutuality and reciprocity in which audiences receive an experience rather than act as participants. This sequestration of experience (Giddens, 1991a) led Thompson to conclude that 'today we live in a world in which the capacity to experience is disconnected from the activity of encountering' (1995, p. 209).

Thompson distances himself from various traditions of critical media research that explain the power of media as resulting from 'an impoverished conception of the self, such as structuralism', which views 'the self ... as a product or construct of the symbolic systems that precede it' (1995, p. 210). Instead, Thompson argues that individuals retain the capacity to construct their selves, and mass communication provides the symbolic resources for the project of the self through which individuals construct a narrative of self-identity over their life trajectory (MacIntyre, 1981). Also, the distant knowledge that supplants local knowledge is often the product of expertise and media production techniques. Media expand the horizons of expectation and enhance the symbolic resources available for self-formation while also placing new demands on the self, combining freedom with media dependency.

The events we observe and experience through the media are distant (Boltanski and Chiapello, 2006; Chouliaraki, 2006) and, therefore, not 'at hand' or 'within reach', and consequently not constituted by recipients' practices. In media culture, the self continuously interweaves with different forms of knowledge and experience, challenging the sense of coherent self-identity and constructing the self through disjointed mediated signs in which little is stable or fixed. Nevertheless, a coherent sense of self can arise from incorporating mediated experiences into the project of the self (MacIntyre, 1981; Giddens, 1991a), which provides a structure of relevance (Schutz, 1967), linking our reception of symbolic material from dispersed and diverse media sources to our everyday life. Thompson (1995) also focuses on the role of the media in reshaping both the relationship between public and private through the reinvention of publicness beyond the state, and the relationship between visibility and invisibility in a media-saturated world. Thompson's account of the relation between media systems, symbolic power and self-formation provides a powerful challenge to Goffman's interactionist account of the self as formed through social interaction. We will return to these questions about the potential interactional affordances of digital media later in this chapter.

BROADCAST TALK AND INFOTAINMENT

In contrast to Thompson's focus on forms of interaction, in which television is portrayed as quasi-social interaction because of its asymmetry and lack of dialogue, there have been studies of the forms of televisual modes of addressing the audience and the development of infotainment genres that, like Twitter (now known as X), are constructed from the interactions of lay participants in media productions, which give some space to the relationship between media and their audiences. In the 1990s, an alternative way of reading and using Goffman's work emerged that applied its sociolinguistic and pragmatic dimensions to the study of broadcast talk (Scannell, 1991). The focus was on how media construct the relationship with their audiences through their mode of address. Scannell and Cardiff (1991) noted that, in its early days, BBC Radio adopted an oratory speaking style. Over time, the BBC came to understand the value of more informal and intimate modes of address, enabling viewers to experience the media as engaging, and engaging them through interaction that created a sense of presence. Influenced by Goffman's focus on interaction as a form of language in action embedded in social practices, Scannell and the other contributors to *Broadcast Talk* (Scannell, 1991) moved away from the model of media as text and reception as reading. Instead, they examined the practical construction of the relationship between media and its audience, understanding media as having a more communicative character akin to face-to-face communication. This focus on language in action informed television and radio analysis of how media construct a sense of liveness even when recorded for later transmission or viewing (Dayan and Katz, 1992). Brand and Scannell (1991) analysed social identity construction over time by media celebrities, creating a sense of a relationship with media audiences. Corner (1991) analysed the news interview as a social occasion, reflecting Goffman's analysis of the staging of social interactions as performances. The study of television 'infotainment genres' in the 1990s was also influenced by Goffman's (1959) analysis of self-presentation, in relation to performance on reality TV (Hill et al., 2005), and by his account of 'footing' (Goffman, 1981), in the analysis of communication frameworks in talk shows (Livingstone and Lunt, 1994). Infotainment signalled a shift in television's generic structure, seeking to engage audiences as media production participants through staged interactional encounters, the development of personal relationships between participants, and confrontation. In her studies of reality TV, Hill shows that performance and authenticity questions are at the heart of audience responses, reflecting Goffman's account of how participants in social interaction observed and judged the credibility and consistency of others' self-presentations (Hill et al., 2005). Reality TV positions the audience as overseeing the interaction, as ratified audiences in Goffman's terms, and their engagement as viewers takes the form of looking for moments of authentic self-presentation or leakages of evidence of intentions or manipulations. This study raises intriguing questions about staging, ritual aspects of communication, authenticity and fresh talk, and the balance between control and spontaneity (Goffman, 1981).

Livingstone and Lunt (1994) used Goffman's analysis of participation frameworks in 'Footing' (1981) to analyse mediated social interaction in talk shows. Taking up the *Broadcast Talk* group's perspective that the media is in a conversation with the audience, they explored the increasing presence of lay members of the public on radio and television, exemplified by the emerging genre of audience discussion programmes or talk shows. A feature of such shows is that there are two audiences, one in the studio and one at home, complicating the forms of address for the talk show host. Livingstone and Lunt explored the interaction between guests, experts and lay participants under the host's direction. The host uses modes of address to create space for participants to contribute to the discussion, protect their voices and ratify studio audience members as participants and observers. The programmes create a context in which participants have equal rights to speak within a structure that starts by making lay experiences visible, elicits expert responses and commentary, and then opens the floor to discussion, debate and argument. The resultant mediated social encounters between the public and various representatives of established power and expertise demonstrate the potential of mediated interaction to bring power to account and provide a voice for those otherwise excluded from public debate. However, talk shows do not constitute a common culture, as suggested by Meyrowitz (1985), and few opportunities for public debate, discussion and argument meet the criteria of a public sphere of discussion and debate as set out by Habermas (1991). Instead, they represent something closer to an oppositional, populist sphere of agonism as suggested by Mouffe (1993), and anticipate the increasingly populist tropes of mainstream media coverage (Lunt, 2019).

FRAMING

Citations of Goffman's *Frame Analysis* (1974) are typical starting points for studies of media frames (Gitlin, 1987; Gamson and Modigliani, 1989; Entman, 1993). Frames organize media contents by selecting information, making specific points salient and using narrative forms that subtly support hegemonic positions on social, political and moral questions. The result is that the viewer, listener or reader is presented with schematically organized, framed information that affords the subtle encoding of ideological and value positions in a way that invites dominant or hegemonic interpretations of the content presented while disguising the framing process. For example, Entman (1993) analysed the framing of information in mainstream media reports of antinuclear movements, demonstrating that the framing made the official government position salient and hid alternative views. Framing is a significant source of the symbolic power of the media to constitute social facts by framing news stories that disguise hegemonic ideological assumptions.

In contrast to the focus on media power and the apparent susceptibility of audiences to framing, in *Frame Analysis* Goffman emphasized the dynamics of frames of interpretation through processes of transformation, keying and lamination. He understood such transformation processes to be a regular part of everyday social interaction as participants reframed, broke frames, rekeyed and shifted the level of abstraction of frames in negotiation or cooperation with other participants. He would have been surprised by the idea of frames being fixed by the media and the view of audiences as passively accepting frames in their interpretation of media content. Consequently, some media researchers approach media framing as including processes of reinterpretation, contestation or opposition by audiences and different social groups or organizations, and as open to influence or contradiction in political debate or opposition, for example, by social movements (Benford and Snow, 2000; Gitlin, 1987). Gamson (1995) argued that there is a dynamic tension between the power of the media to frame media contents and the possibility of reframing or subversive action from audiences and interest groups.

There is no consensus about the balance between hegemonic media power and the various tactics used to disrupt it. Entman (1993) focused on the power of the media to frame information and communicate established interpretations of reported events. In contrast, Gamson et al. (1992) and Benford (2013) emphasized how frames are open to interpretation, transformation and counter-framing. Characteristically, Goffman explored both these perspectives on framing: 'my aim is to try to isolate some of the basic frameworks of understanding available in our society for making sense out of events and to analyse the special vulnerabilities to which these frames of reference are subject' (1974, p. 10). The field debates the balance between the media's capacity to fix frames of interpretation and their openness to interpretation and contestation. Goffman implied that all frames were vulnerable to reinterpretation and practices of contestation or disruption, implying limits to media power: 'Goffman was concerned with the conditions under which people challenge existing rules of interaction, and he recognised the stake of authorities in maintaining such rules. In addition, he was concerned with the conditions under which people became aware of inequality and differences. In this sense, his agenda was implicitly political' (Gamson, 1985, p. 609).

Goffman's ideas about framing are compatible with developments in social movements, especially those that are international in scope and realize the energies of popular political movements such as environmentalism. In this, contesting frameworks of interpretation in the mainstream media have changed political consciousness. Similarly, the individualization of political engagement has been accompanied by a proliferation of the politics of disruption, including contesting frames (Isin and Ruppert, 2020). These dynamics are emergent and contrast with traditional understandings of social movements that gain support and work as collectives.

DIGITALLY MEDIATED INTERACTION:
BLURRING THE PUBLIC AND PRIVATE

Thompson (2018) revisited his work on the media and modernity in the context of the expanded interactional affordances of digital media. In addition to his previous taxonomy of forms of social interaction as face-to-face interaction, mediated interaction and mediated quasi-interaction, he recognized that digital media, in contrast to mass media, afford the potential for digitally mediated interaction in a many-to-many form of communication.

To illustrate the broader social significance of digitally mediated interaction, Thompson revisited Goffman's distinction between frontstage and backstage as regions of social life. Goffman explored the fragility of the interaction order, including the spilling of information 'given off' through the inopportune revelation of secrets or the leaking of non-verbal cues in the proximity of social interaction (Goffman, 1959). Thompson argues that the mixture of mass communication and digitally mediated communication transforms the field of politics 'so that political life now unfolds in an information environment that is difficult to control, creating a permanently unstable arena in which leaks, revelations and disclosures are always capable of disrupting the most well-laid plans' (2018, p. 1). These circumstances lead to a transformation of visibility that creates new forms of fragility in public life in which participants face increasing risks and forms of disruption (Isin, 2008; Lunt, 2020). This new fragility is enhanced by the massively expanded accessibility and searchability of extensive stores of digital content (Baym, 2015) in a context in which institutional gatekeepers are less effective and there is the potential for anyone to be a source of public information: 'The banalisation of recording coupled with the democratisation of transmission means that social and political life is now awash with digitised symbolic content that outstrips, at an ever-increasing pace, the ability of any individual or organisation to control it' (Thompson, 2018, p. 22).

Consequently, public figures, including politicians, are perpetually vulnerable to exposure, critique and scandal since what in the past might have stayed secret is made visible, leading to potential public ridicule and outrage. The potential risks are not only reputational but also affect democratic processes of accountability, persuasion and voting in the political process. Political scandals remind 'us all of just how fragile this arena now is, just how fluid the boundary between public and private life has now become and just how important it is for us as social scientists to try to understand this turbulent new world of mediated visibility in the digital age' (Thompson, 2018, p. 25). This blurring of boundaries between public and private and the fragility of digital life contrasts with Goffman's (1959) account of the barriers between social life regions and his analysis of the strategies that individuals and groups used to manage threats and mishaps. These points related to the mediation of self-formation, the increased visibility of everyday life and the democratization of symbolic resources for broadcasting the self through digital and social media will be explored later in this chapter.

PLATFORM PARTICIPATION: INFLUENCERS AND DIGITAL PUBLICS

Marwick and boyd (2011) characterize Twitter as a social media environment that constitutes a hyperextension of Meyrowitz's (1985) idea of a common culture. Social media also democratizes the 'broadcasting' of messages across potentially vast networks of contacts and contacts of contacts in a many-to-many communication form. In addition, Twitter contacts consist of a mixture of friends, relations, acquaintances, work colleagues and strangers, constituting a collapsed context in which contacts of all kinds inhabit the same space. Marwick and boyd recognize that this collapsed context presents a significant challenge to participants in framing their tweets because all communication is, to some degree, tailored to an intended or imagined audience. In the face-to-face encounters studied by Goffman, there were many cues as to fellow participants' social roles, characters, interests and motivations, and the local context of the encounters also constrained the diversity of participants. In face-to-face social encounters, contextual and interactional cues allow participants to adapt their self-presentations to fit the context, situation and audience (Goffman, 1959). Many of these cues are missing on Twitter, so addressing the audience for posts requires an act of imagining that audience. Users must attune to their 'sense' of the potential audience and bring it into being through how they draft their posts.

Marwick and boyd conducted an online survey of Twitter users to see how, in these circumstances, they configured the imagined audiences for their posts and how this was reflected in their communication strategies when framing tweets and other interventions in the Twittersphere. The survey explicitly asked who the participants imagined reading their tweets, who they tweeted to, and what made an individual seem authentic on Twitter. Their sample included 'power users' who had over 100,000 followers and followed few people, and more everyday users with fewer followers and more of a balance between followers and followed in their contacts.

The question about who was addressed by tweets brought a range of responses, including social categories of 'friends', 'fans' and 'myself'. In some cases, offline friends and associates were also friends on Twitter. Interestingly, some users said that the platform provided a 'live diary to all my friends, posting what they might find interesting' (Marwick and boyd, 2011, p. 118). Others claimed not to be concerned about the potential audience for tweets and regarded Twitter as a 'me' space of personal expression. Some were uncomfortable using the term 'audience' and rejected the idea of self-publicity or personal branding as a motivation for tweeting. Other respondents bought into the strategic use of tweets to recruit and maintain followers. These observations led to interpretations that speak to an ideology of publicity, promotion and the commodification of the self, as identified in studies of micro-celebrity and influencers (Marwick, 2013, 2020; van Dijck, 2013). Marwick and boyd compared users who are oriented towards consociates such as friends, family and coworkers, and those who seek to establish a fan base or contribute to developing an online community. These different audiences are addressed in the uniform environment of Twitter mainly through different modes of address (Livingstone and Lunt, 1994). For example, insider knowledge is used in tweets to address some participants and exclude others, a strategy that Goffman (1959) discusses concerning teamwork in the performance of self-presentation (see also Chen and Lunt, 2021). Posts vary in terms of whether they seek to address a particular audience or are floated into the air (Peters, 1999).

Marwick and boyd focused their analysis on micro-celebrities with large followings who use strategies to attract a broad audience with varied tastes and preferences. As influencers, they provide commentary and tweet on a wide range of topics to attract and retain a following. However, those seeking and sustaining a large audience have various motives and strategies, including using Twitter as a broadcast medium (one-to-many), as a marketing channel, as a diary, as a social platform for issues or interests and as a news source

(Marwick and boyd, 2011). Strategies to build followers employ populist rhetoric, including the use of terms such as 'we' and 'us', and empty signifiers or codes that are open to interpretation from a variety of perspectives. The analysis reveals a distinction, maybe a tension, between users becoming or aiming to become influencers and those participants who, 'with few followers, . . . use the site for reasons other than self-promotion, generally . . . as a personal space where spam, advertising, and marketing are unwelcome' (Marwick and boyd, 2011, p. 124). However, if we think of these communications as establishing and sustaining forms of sociality, we can think of many reasons for engagement with Twitter other than promoting the self. Visibility can serve many purposes, including establishing identity or reputational claims, participating in public life and intervening in debates and discussions as a form of interest and entertainment.

A significant element of the interaction order articulated by Goffman is that of civil inattention in public encounters, which Marwick and boyd identify through examples of self-censorship on Twitter. In civil inattention, people flatten out their communications to avoid bringing attention to themselves in public, allowing others to get on with their legitimate business while being open to involvement in interaction. Civil inattention goes against the grain of those seeking to exploit social media's information economy and aiming for visible self-promotion. Another contrast is a commitment to treating social media as a space of public deliberation and debate, providing opinions or commentary on events in a marketplace of ideas (Geuss, 2001). The civility dimension of this is reinforced by Marwick and boyd's finding that potentially controversial topics, such as dating, sex, relationships and marital problems, are not often aired on Twitter, suggesting some norms of civility.

There is a parallel between Goffman's comparison of professional actors with the amateur dramatics of everyday life and the coexistence on Twitter of micro-celebrities and users engaged in various purposes and social relations. Micro-celebrities represent an extreme formulation of the marketing of the self, alongside which there are more everyday ways in which people promote the self or use the platform to sustain social relationships, support causes, engage in public discussion and debate, and so on. Twitter can accommodate radically contrasting and complicated forms of engagement and action (Boyd, 2014). What kind of place is a platform like Twitter? A city, a map, a language, a bazaar, a supermarket of ideas – not unlike Goffman's perception of the society he studied as constituted by multiple realities or regions of social life sustained through interaction.

In *Twitter: A Biography*, Burgess and Baym (2020) trace the development of Twitter, emphasizing the ambiguity of the meanings and social roles played out on a platform that supports a diversity of uses and cultural forms, including mediated personal social relations and public discussion. They document the tensions between media reports of Twitter and academic accounts of the richness, openness and diversity of users engaging the platform and its various emergent cultures. They argue that there is a tension between a technology of everyday life in which one connects with friends and a public communication platform (Burgess and Baym, 2020).

HYPERCONNECTIVITY AND THE SELF

The theme of the self in the digital age is explored by Brubaker, who argues that the digital affords new ways of 'being and constructing a self [and] ... new ways in which selves are configured, represented and governed by sociotechnical systems' (2020, p. 76). He links the analysis of the social self to the structure–agency question in the context of powerful digital corporations, the saturation of everyday life by media culture, and the new potentials that digital media provide for the expression and constitution of the self. Digital industries, technologies and cultures have 'engendered new ways of objectifying, quantifying, producing and regulating the self' (Brubaker, 2020, p. 771). Digital media afford new opportunities for self-expression, sociality and, simultaneously, new forms of objectification.

In mapping out a sociology of hyperconnectivity, Brubaker draws on Goffman's analysis of self-presentation but significantly also on several social theoretical resources. The crucial element contributed by Goffman is the view that self-formation is a social phenomenon that is 'formed and sustained through ongoing social interaction and performative enactment' (Brubaker, 2020, p. 772). Brubaker complements these ideas from Goffman with the sociology of reflexive modernity and the idea of the project of the self and reflexivity based on continuous self-monitoring (Giddens, 1991a). In this view, social relationships are formed as conjoint projects of the self and sustained or ceased according to the value they bring to participants. Individuals draw on the widespread availability of information and advice sources and social institutions' attunement to the project of reflexive modernity and new forms of individualization characterized by institutional reflexivity (Beck and Beck-Gernsheim, 2002). Digital media potentially transform the project of the self by providing powerful new tools for self-monitoring and self-knowledge, expanding the potential of such resources compared to Giddens's (1991a) account of the role of self-help books as resources for the project of the self.

The resources available to individuals in a digitally mediated environment include algorithms attuned to people's preferences and choices, and devices that provide real-time digitally mediated feedback on their activities and social connections both offline and online. In addition, the accessibility of a vast knowledge resource intensifies and immediately makes available analytics of social trends, commentary and diverse views on all aspects of social and cultural life, creating hyper-reflexivity. Brubaker (2020) also draws on Foucault's (1990) late work on technologies of the self as disciplinary practices in conjunction with reflexive practices of the care of the self. These ideas invite the study of the way that digital technologies are implicated in the dispersal of disciplinary practices that operate on the body, as well as psychological techniques of control and self-control, and raise questions about the ways that digital technologies extend disciplinary power while also providing resources for the care of the self and forms of relationship and autonomy that resist or obviate the potential for capture by the purposes of digital corporations. Brubaker suggests a range of dialectic relationships between new horizons of experience in the infosphere (Floridi, 2014), as post-traditional forms of life reduce the salience of communities of origin and the associated normative obligations placed on individuals (Brubaker, 2020, p. 778). Following Mead's (1934), Bateson's (1973) and Goffman's (1961b) analysis of the role of play in social identity through which we experience an objectified self, engagements in social media may be seriously playful, enhancing self-consciousness through awareness of how we appear to others. Simultaneously, the quantified self in data-driven life standardizes everyday practices through regimes of the scrutiny of the self, and lays down records and traces of activities that contribute to the observation and surveillance of everyday life practices.

However, Brubaker also argues that digital forms of knowing the self provide resources for governing the self as projects that are played out in and adapted to social media ecology. He discusses Marwick's work on new forms of micro-celebrity as paradigmatic of new forms of self-enterprise, 'producing and enacting a digital self that succeeds in engaging and being consumed by followers' (2013, p. 17). Brubaker complements the Goffmanian account of the expressive performance of the self with Rose's (1999) account of the enterprising self that makes choices with a heightened sense of psychological awareness, along with Giddens's (1991a) account of self-monitoring, self-authoring and reflexive identity. Traditionally, these accounts are understood as alternative visions of the self in the modern age. Brubaker, however, understands these approaches as complementary analyses of new forms and opportunities for governing the self. The self does realize itself as an entrepreneur or consumer but also as embedded in expanded forms of sociality and as realizing a reflexive identity. In everyday life, digital media also provide resources for regulating moods and bodily states and inducing pleasurable experiences through, for example, access to music and digital devices that monitor various bodily functions (Brubaker, 2020). The data are available to sociotechnical systems which, using algorithms, can regulate and recommend what we watch, read and listen to, or provide a continuous background of sounds and images alongside forms of knowledge and experience (Hepp, 2020).

These accounts of governing and regulating the self in a digital environment reassert but do not resolve the tensions between media-enhanced reflexive and algorithmically guided practices. Similar tensions exist in Foucault's account of technologies of the self and the care of the self. Digital self-governing points to new modalities in which these tensions arise, between enterprise, responsibility and discipline (Brubaker, 2020).

CONCLUSION

Goffman's work has been a resource for media studies in relation to public media that addresses its audience through participation in the hybrid genres of infotainment, mobile phones, social media and online platforms. Various themes in media sociology (Waisbord, 2014) are engaged in these studies of the social implications of the interaction order, illustrating Goffman's eclectic engagement with different sociological theories and perspectives, including Durkheim's sociology of religion, neo-Durkheimian theory, reflexive modernity theory, Bourdieu's analysis of symbolic power, political economy, Foucault's accounts of disciplinary power and his late work on technologies and care of the self. In addition, various perspectives on media theory are evident, across a variety of media technologies of mass communication and digital media. Several of Goffman's key ideas are represented, including self-presentation and dramaturgy, communication frameworks and framing. Goffman is indeed a resource for different areas of media studies. What is visible is the alacrity with which media scholars and sociologists with an interest in the role of the media in modernity adapt Goffman's work to various perspectives to address different sociological questions.

What themes of media sociology are addressed by these various studies that engage Goffman's work? The social effects of media cultures take several forms, creating and shaping a common culture but also providing resources for self-formation and the project of the self, reconfiguring the relation between public and private, home and public life. Links have been established between Goffman's work and questions of social solidarity, with different accounts of what connects the micro-work of social interaction and the macro-view of social cohesion. A key concern is the increased visibility that is part of the mediatization of everyday life, including problems of public exposure, and there is a tension between accounts of the liberalizing effects of media culture and its implications for the enrolment of subjectivity in processes of social control. Another critical theme is self-formation, in which powerful media seek to maximize attention and profit from participants while providing the resources for entrepreneurialism and engagement in social life and the pursuit of social causes. The work also maps the development of media systems and technologies from the television age through digital media to platformization.

In Chapter 5, these themes and questions around the elision of Goffman's work with sociological and media theories are taken up in the study of contemporary media in relation to media rituals, practice and the process of mediatization.

5

CONCLUSIONS

INTRODUCTION

In this concluding chapter, I discuss the potential of Goffman's work to contribute to key themes in media research and the emerging field of digital sociology with a focus on how his writings might inform discussions of the relationship between everyday life, self-formation and media as a sociotechnical system (Brubaker, 2020). I also reflect on the implications of the engagement with Goffman's writings, which are reviewed in this book as an example of the interdisciplinary relation between media studies and sociology (Waisbord, 2014). In Chapter 3, we saw examples of how ideas from Goffman's work have been taken up in the study of mediated social interaction, qualifying his distinction between face-to-face encounters and mediated social interaction. In Chapter 4, we looked at various ways of linking Goffman's ideas to sociological and media theory in the context of studies of the blurring of the boundary between public and private, the availability of expanded forms of digital connection, sociability and practice beyond local contexts, and the increased potential of resources for self-formation, management and governance by individuals and sociotechnical systems.

The applications of Goffman's ideas in the study of the media we have reviewed in this book create a context for rethinking the interrelation between mediated social interaction and sociotechnical systems. As we have seen, the development of digital media has given new impetus to interest in Goffman's work in media studies, resulting from the radical expansion of connectivity across time and space and the interactional affordances of digital media compared to those available in Goffman's day. In this chapter, I focus on media as a sociotechnical system to discuss the potential relevance of Goffman's ideas to the changing context of the mediation of everything (Livingstone, 2009), synergizing with the fields of media phenomenology, rituals and practice, and the spread of media to all aspects of social life through mediatization. I finish with a synthesis of key ideas from the book as a framework for understanding the role of mediated social interaction and system integration as articulated by Giddens (1984), and argue for a recognition of the increasing significance of the media as a sociotechnical system in understanding everyday life and its relation to broader social structures, systems and processes.

I have chosen Giddens's (1984) structuration theory as a framework because it is an exemplary attempt to integrate Goffman's writings with social theory and to analyse the relationship between social and systems integration. Giddens (1984, 1991a) has done more than most social theorists to fill the theoretical gaps in Goffman's writings and to link his account of the interaction order with broader sociological questions in a way that has been influential in the study of media and modernity (Thompson, 1995) and mediatization (Hjarvard, 2013). However, questions are raised for structuration by the emergence of powerful digital media companies, by the capability of media technologies and systems to penetrate everyday life, and by the access they provide to users in expanded networks of connection and social knowledge. These changes suggest new ways of thinking about the ethics of interaction orders, the constitution of public order and civility, the experience of intersubjectivity, and the social significance of the constitutive practices in everyday life in the context of the development of digital media as powerful sociotechnical systems.

I also explore the relationship between Goffman's work and digital sociology (Daniels et al., 2017; Zukin and Torpey, 2020). The rapid growth, global reach, and power of the tech giants, and the spread of digital media technologies across institutions and everyday life practices, all raise important questions for media studies and the emerging digital sociology field. However, while media scholars have been quick to engage with the radical, transformative potential of the spread of media into all areas of social life and culture, there has been more circumspection in sociology. For example, Zukin and Torpey reflect on the challenges involved in incorporating the study of emerging digital technologies and cultures into sociology in a way that recognizes the complexity of the digital while linking it to 'classical sociology's concern with the state, the self, knowledge, and power' (2020, p. 745). Partly, this caution reflects arguments developed in the social studies of science and technology against technological determinism (MacKenzie and Wajcman, 1998; Zukin and Torpey, 2020). In addition, established traditions of sociological research – for example, on the transition to post-industrial society (Bell, 1976) – anticipate social transformations that overlap with the claims of the digital network society. Similarly, various approaches to understanding modernity that emphasize the emptying out of the nation-state, the increasing importance of the local and the global, and the transitions to late modern, reflexive modernity (Giddens, 1991a) also anticipate many of the claims made for digital culture and society. In this context, Torpey (2020) suggests two agendas for digital sociology: one focusing on the power of digital corporations, the other on digital media and everyday life. The first recognizes the 'power of Big Tech companies, which have increasingly dominated the economic landscape, and their creators, owners and investors'; the second offers a complementary agenda focused on 'transforming everyday life due to the spread of new technologies' (Torpey, 2020, p. 75). This latter aspect of digital sociology includes the implications of mobility for social relations (Ling, 2008), the potential for deliberation, being caught up in an attention economy, and the contrast between pessimistic and optimistic accounts of digital culture and everyday life.

In linking Goffman's work to these themes and research agendas, I make an argument for the continuing relevance of his writings and echo his persistent calls for the recognition of the paramount importance of everyday life in understanding society, his focus on social interaction as a critical site of social and cultural processes (Mische, 2011), his recognition of agency even in the darkest places, and his acceptance of the necessity of engaging multiple perspectives in understanding social being (Goffman, 1983).

MEDIATED SOCIAL INTERACTION AS EXPERIENCE, RITUAL, SOCIAL PRACTICE AND MEDIATIZATION

In response to the recent transformations in media technologies and systems, various approaches have developed within media and communication that have unsettled the theories and approaches established in the age of linear media (Couldry and Hepp, 2013). Echoing Goffman's description of his work as sniping at a target from different perspectives, I seek to explore the overlaps and resonances as well as the differences between Goffman's ideas and media research on these topics that has not always explicitly acknowledged his work. For example, approaches to media phenomenology resonate with Goffman's debt to Schutz's social phenomenology; the analysis of media and practice with Goffman's understanding of the interaction order as a practical accomplishment and constitutive practice (Rawls, 2012); the analysis of media rituals (Couldry, 2002) with Goffman's (1967) engagement with the ritual organization of social encounters. There are also overlaps with the process sociology inherent in theories of social networks and mediatization (Mische, 2011; Hepp, 2020).

Media phenomenology

Goffman's work mainly focused on the forms of interaction in social encounters, an essential element of which was the organization of experience (Goffman, 1974; Persson, 2022). In *Frame Analysis* (1974), Goffman cited and discussed Schutz's (1967) phenomenology partly in response to the centrality of Schutz's work in Berger and Luckmann's *The Social Construction of Reality* (1966). Goffman sought an alternative account of social constructionism based on interactionism, and responded to the criticism of his own work's lack of explicit engagement with theory. There has been some scepticism as to the relevance of phenomenology for understanding Goffman's writings (Smith, 2006; Jacobsen and Kristiansen, 2010). However, in this section, I analyse the resonances between Goffman's analysis of the interaction

order and Schutz's social phenomenology as an account of
the paramount reality of the lifeworld (Eberle, 2012) and, by
extension, of media life (Deuze, 2012). There are two significant ways in which Goffman's writing was influenced
by Schutz: in identifying different orientations to others in
social encounters, and in navigating a social world constituted by multiple realities.

At the start of his account of directly experienced social
reality, Schutz examined different ways of orienting oneself
towards others in social encounters in which participants
are 'in reach of each other's direct experience ... in the
"face-to-face" situation' (1967, p. 163). In such encounters,
participants can directly experience and share 'a community
of space and time' as a fundamental aspect of social life (Ayaß,
2014). Goffman's work on the interaction order examined
concrete instances of these fundamental encounters through
his observation and interpretation of copresent, face-to-face
social situations in which participants' experience was organized.

Schutz's analysis of copresent social encounters distinguished between orientations towards others as 'mere objects'
and engagements that make an existential commitment to
others as subjects or as conscious, intelligent social beings
(Crossley, 1996, p. 79). Goffman drew similar distinctions
between the coordination of action according to 'traffic rules',
such as avoiding bumping into others in the street, coordination of action in a ritual or in staging a play, various forms
of social influence and conversations as mutually constituted
experience. Where Schutz (1967) distinguished between
'Other-orientation' and 'affecting the other', or social influence in our orientation to others, Goffman (1959) similarly
differentiated social interaction aimed at influencing others
– not least in inducing favourable impressions in them – from
more collaborative interactions based on shared experience.

Schutz also contrasted social action as coordination or social influence with social relations exemplified by conversations in which we are oriented to constituting meanings through reciprocity (1967, p. 163). This form of intersubjectivity realized through social interaction has salient features: 'The face-to-face relationship in which the partners are aware of each other and sympathetically participate in each other's lives for however short a time we call the "pure We-relationship"' (1967, p. 164). The We-relationship goes beyond individual consciousness to include the body and a shared stream of consciousness or attunement, which Schutz illustrated through the example of making music together. When we participate in such shared experiences, we stay engaged in the joint practice, which we must step out of in order to reflect on it. Goffman (1959) applied these ideas in his analysis of cooperative teamwork, identifying appropriate levels of attention, reflection and metacommunication, and displays of loyalty and commitment to the shared impression evoked by the group, along with tact.

Goffman's writings analysed these various relationships in concrete social reality, in which the We-relationship is realized through mutual gaze and the reciprocal organization of interaction and conversation. Concrete We-relationships 'may be experienced with different degrees of immediacy, intensity, or intimacy' (Schutz, 1967, p. 168), which is reflected in Goffman's analysis of the organization of encounters as centre and periphery, requiring the integration of different points of view and levels of involvement and attention (1963b).

Schutz's account of the realization of the We-relationship in everyday social encounters involved a communicative style that is also reflected in Goffman's analysis of the experience of social encounters: 'For the participants, this involves a single vision and cognitive focus of attention, a moral and preferential openness to verbal communication, a heightened mutual relevance of acts, and an eye-to-eye ecological huddle that maximizes each participant's opportunity to perceive the other participants' monitoring of him. Given these communication arrangements, their presence must be acknowledged or ratified through expressive signs, and a "we rationale" is likely to emerge' (Goffman, 1961b, p. 18).

Schutz also anticipated Goffman's dramaturgical metaphor: 'The world of everyday life is the scene and object of our actions and interactions. We have to dominate it, and we have to change it in order to realize the purposes that we pursue within it among our fellow men. We work and operate within and upon the world' (1967, pp. 208f). Goffman was not writing phenomenology but applying Schutz's analysis of the phenomenology of social life to 'concrete individuals with flesh and blood, who act based on their intentions, play different roles in different settings and who have a personal identity, a biography and plans for the future' (Eberle, 2012, p. 290).

How does this phenomenological reading of Goffman's analysis of experience in social interactions relate to media phenomenology (Markham and Rodgers, 2017)? Screen media and, perhaps even more so, social media can be understood as forming part of 'the taken-for-granted stream of everyday routines, interactions and events that constitute both individual and social experience' (Markham and Rodgers, 2017, p. 6). The idea that media create a horizon for human experience – a world into which we throw ourselves, experience ourselves and realize our futures as a way of being in the world – appears increasingly relevant as media are seen as part of the environment within which everyday life unfolds.

Goffman's analysis of the interaction order incorporated the idea that face-to-face social encounters take place within, but also constitute, this taken-for-granted stream of everyday routines, interactions and events. For the most part, however, media phenomenology has yet to concern itself with the analysis of participation and interaction, focusing instead on how the media shapes or configures experience. Scannell (2014), for example, focuses on how radio and television production is grounded in already existing shared ideas and meanings, providing a context for media audiences. Sobchack (1992) similarly locates the film viewer in 'compositions, editing, framings, points of view' which 'construct a lived space experienced by a film body whose effects resonate in that of the viewer' (quoted in Andiloro, 2023, p. 3). As Markham and Rodgers (2017) suggest, a key strand of media phenomenology emphasizes how media shapes and structures experience. The role of participants in constructing the media environment and the experience of engagement and reception of media suggests a Schutzian social phenomenology as a potentially fruitful interpretation of Goffman's work and its application in the study of the role of participants in shaping the environment of digital and social media.

Media rituals

In Chapter 4, we debated whether the social bonds established and reinforced through mobile phone connection constituted ceremonial or ritual forms of engagement. The study of media rituals is another area where insights from Goffman's analysis of the relationship between rituals, recognition and civility offer new insights. Couldry (2002) offers the most developed analysis of media rituals, engaging with the complex arguments about ritual in anthropology in order to abstract from them an understanding of media ritual. My argument here is focused on Goffman's (1967) analysis of interaction rituals and its potential relevance for under-

standing media rituals. I say 'potential' because, as we saw
in Ling's (2008) analysis, Goffman has commonly been associated with Durkheim's (1995 [1912]) study of ritual in the
context of ceremonies, an approach that has been compre-
hensively explored by Rothenbuhler (1998) and is reflected
in Couldry's account.

Couldry (2002) criticizes the transcendent aspects of ceremony, as depicted in Durkheim's work and in Rothenbuhler's
analysis of mediated ceremonies. In Durkheim's account,
ceremonial rituals are understood as puncturing the banal
routines of everyday life through episodes of collective effervescence organized around the valorization of a sacred totem
as a symbol of the clan, group or society. In contrast, Couldry
prefers Turner's (1977, 1982) analysis of ritual as liminality,
which focuses on transitions between social categories as the
heart of ritual rather than a relation to a transcendent reality
that punctuates the routines of everyday life.

I argued in Chapter 4, however, that although Goffman
(1967) invoked Durkheim in his study of rituals in
everyday life, he did not do so concerning collective representations and ceremonies. Goffman was more influenced
by Durkheim's understanding of rituals as rites that govern
access to and deportment towards the totem outside of ceremonial contexts as part of the routines of everyday life.
He followed Durkheim's analysis of the limits of consensus
in the complex, pluralistic societies of modernity in which
social solidarity is formed through recognizing others in
everyday forms of civility. Consequently, Goffman regarded
everyday salutations as a kind of care based on recognizing
the common humanity in self and others, which, rather than
symbolizing the collective, references principles of human
rights and democratic governance. Conventions of politeness
in social interactions are interpreted as organic solidarity
reproducing a culture of civility rather than as symbolic of

collectives, consensus or shared social norms and cultural values.

Goffman (1967) analysed concrete instances in everyday social encounters that reflected the realization of the sacred as a recognition of rights-bearing individuals in the mundane, ritual commonplaces of greeting, turn-taking and conversation as face-work. He complemented this by analysing how participants protect the space for civil engagement. If there is a deity, it is that element of human existence that connects us and can only thrive in the context of the recognition of human rights and democratic institutions. Had Goffman witnessed the panoply of contemporary digital media, he might have found resonances with this conception of ritual, which contrasts with ceremony as transcendence. This approach also makes possible an understanding of social categories not as ceremonially authenticated but as arising in social encounters, even mediated ones (Rawls, 2012).

Media and practice

The study of media as practice is another area of media theory that overlaps with Goffman's work in potentially interesting ways. Postill defines practice in the introduction to *Theorising Media and Practice* in a way that could well be used to describe Goffman's account of how social interaction is played out by flawed participants in the routines of everyday life: 'Practices are embedded sets of activities that humans perform with varying degrees of regularity, competence and flair' (Bräuchler and Postill, 2010, p. 1). Postill recognizes the study of media anthropology as having explored media practices in various contexts. Goffman does not, however, appear in the book's index and is not recognized as engaging with the study of social practice. I will outline how an engagement with Goffman's work might contribute to the analysis of media practices first by drawing out the interactional aspects of media practice in Postill's introduction and then by discussing Rawls' (2012) analysis of Goffman's understanding of constitutive practices and its potential for the study of media practices.

Couldry (2004) called for a new media research paradigm based on the analysis of practice in sociology, one which would shift media and communication away from a focus on the analysis of texts and interpretations and the political economy of media industries. Setting aside the somewhat hyperbolic claims for a new paradigm, bringing media research into contact with both practice theory and sociology was prescient given the encroaching digital age and the spread of media into everyday life and institutional contexts. Postill points out that although there is a development of interest in practice in media research, the term itself has often been taken for granted. He seeks to provide an account of the philosophical origins of practice theory in sociology and its applications in media anthropology as a foundation for the study of media practice (Bräuchler and Postill, 2010). For example, Wittgenstein (1953) and Bourdieu (1977) are invoked as laying the ground for practice theory, reflecting Bourdieu's (1990) critique of the dichotomy of objectivism and subjectivism in social theory in which Goffman is allocated to the ranks of subjectivist theories (which partly explains his absence in the book).

How can Goffman's writings be defended against the charge of subjectivism and aligned with the theory of practice, asserting a role for interactionism in the study of media practice (Lunt, 2020)? One route is to recognize Goffman's writing as identifying a dynamic between constraint and freedom and between conformity to rules, roles and moral values and self-regulatory social practices (Rawls, 2012). Rawls traces the idea of constitutive practice back to Durkheim's distinction between traditional forms of social practice and constitutive social practices. In contrast to the idea that social order is the product of collective representations as shared social norms and cultural values, constitutive practices link individual freedom and agency to social structure. Goffman's analysis of social interaction revealed 'constitutive, spontaneous and self-regulating practices' in everyday life (Rawls, 2012, p. 480). Rawls argues that participation in networks of practices requires openness of participation, voluntarism and self-regulation, reflecting both Goffman's analysis of teamwork in *The Presentation of Self in Everyday Life* and his account of the way social interaction creates the contexts for recognition and civility (Geuss, 2001). Rawls also draws on Durkheim to argue that such commitments to work with others in the constitution of social practices imply an orientation to social justice and a moral dimension of reciprocal forms of social interaction that complements accounts based on regulation by authority or formal rules. Similarly, Goffman recognizes a form of social solidarity based on trust and reciprocity: 'The constitutive practice argument requires that there be essential moral obligations of reciprocity, attention, and competence necessarily involved in orienting practices in sufficient detail' (Rawls, 2012, p. 283).

Rawls (2022) argues that Goffman's Jewish identity made him aware of everyday processes of social exclusion and the consequent limits of consensus over social norms and cultural values. The critical point is that 'practices and their constitutive requirements can replace consensus as the means for creating Individual/Self and social coherence in modernity' (Rawls, 2022, p. 35). In this way, Durkheim and, in following him, Goffman turned individualization on its head by arguing that it afforded, through social interaction and intersubjectivity, the potential for constitutive practices that afford self-formation and generate social facts and social solidarity.

The affordances of digital media in everyday life and informal orders in institutional contexts reflect Goffman's (1959) view of the incursion of interaction orders into other forms of social order. In digital media, there is a dynamic tension between performance as an expressive self, which assumes an already constituted self, and 'digital media [which] potentially provides a neutral stage for interaction and a matrix of co-constitutive practices' (Siles, 2017, p. 192).

Mediatization

Mediatization theory combines elements of media logic (Altheide and Snow, 1979) with the mediation of everything (Livingstone, 2008). It seeks to understand how media spreads and provides the infrastructure for all aspects of society and culture. It has been widely applied in, for example, studies of the mediatization of politics, organizations, law, art and popular culture (Lundby, 2014). As an emerging field of media research, mediatization has been at the core of debates which turn on a broad distinction between approaches that focus on the spread of the logics of mediation into institutional contexts (Hjarvard, 2013) and those that focus on the mediatization of the social and cultural dimensions of everyday life (Couldry and Hepp, 2013). These different perspectives on mediatization took as their starting points different sociologies. Hepp and Couldry (2013; see also Couldry and Hepp, 2017), for instance, combined elements of Elias's (2000) theory of social structures as figurations with elements of social constructionism (Berger and Luckmann, 1966) to study the involvement of media in social processes that intertwine configurations of individuals and social and cultural forms in a mediated construction of reality. In contrast, Hjarvard (2013) draws on Giddens's (1984) structuration theory to argue for a perspective on the historical development of media conceived initially as instruments of established social and cultural forms, then as cultural institutions in their own right (exemplified by public service media serving the nation), and finally, in the context of contemporary media systems, as relatively independent institutions integrated into other social institutions and systems. Hjarvard offers a functional analysis that owes much to theories of media logic (Altheide and Snow, 1979), arguing that media shape social life by intervening in social interaction and communications between institutions (Hjarvard, 2013, p. 27).

However, there has been a comparative neglect of the individual, social encounters and social relationships in accounts of mediatization, as the focus has been on understanding how the demands of promotion in an expanding media environment influence institutional and individual self-promotion and the logic of social action. What is the equivalent of active audience interpretation of linear media contents or participation in co-production in the theory of media audiences (Livingstone, 2005; Schröder, 2017)? Hepp (2020) explores the embedding of individuals in the multiple configurations of what he calls 'deep mediatization', including the organization of media viewing alongside the proliferation of the datafication of the self through digital spaces and the spread of 'interveillance'. Following Elias's (2000) analysis of the duality of individual and social configurations, Hepp examines the embedding of individuals in an increasingly complex media environment that shapes and provides resources for structuring, managing and governing the self. Elias had sought to overcome the classic distinction between structure and agency, and Hepp works through the implications of how media constitute expanded resources for individuals in self-formation and governance in dynamic, mediatized social environments. Individuals are formed in the context of the dynamic social relationships, friendship groups and institutions they are involved with. Hepp argues that these configuration processes are now significantly played out through the media as deep mediatization.

Hepp acknowledges the parallels between Elias's process theory of the interaction between individual and social configurations and Goffman's analysis of self-formation as 'continuously created in and through the situations in which people find themselves' such that it 'is neither static nor coherent' (Hepp, 2020, p. 150). However, the role of individuals in social configurations and the resulting habitus (Bourdieu, 1990) is described as one in which individuals are oriented toward and embedded, implicated or involved in social configurations. In his study of self-tracking through wearable devices in practices such as exercising and dieting, Hepp emphasizes the ambivalence of the practical utility of these devices in terms of the level of control they afford the user in exchange for data open to exploitation. His study mainly focuses on individual self-formation and social configurations that include groups, communities and big tech companies (Hepp, 2020, p. 161). From an interactionist perspective, accounts of self-tracking predominantly articulate a relationship between individuals and generalized others in the forms of data doubles and the various virtual communities of practice established in the applications used to set standards as part of exercise routines. This account extends our understanding of individualization in the context of surveillance technologies (Dencik, 2018) and the associated resignation in the face of datafication. These themes are discussed in the next section, in relation to the role of interaction in mediated self-formation in the context of powerful media, in which Goffman's writing plays an important part.

In mediatization (Hepp, 2020; Hjarvard, 2013), the spread of media through social systems and everyday life has been claimed to constitute an autonomous sociological meta-process (Krotz, 2007). However, in deference to the long-run sociological metaprocesses of individualization, rationaliza-tion, globalization, urbanization, innovation and the social shaping of technology, we might think of how the mediation of everything and mediatization intersect with these sociolog-ical metaprocesses. For example, concerning social processes of self-formation, a variety of conceptions of the self that are not reducible to traditional notions of individualization have emerged, including the reflexive self, the project of the self and the datafied self, all of which are fuelled by media. Mediatization also intersects and intensifies processes of self-formation because these changes are both driven by the development of powerful media corporations and simultane-ously provide widespread access to radically advanced forms of knowledge. These are resources that go well beyond the framing of social interaction. Consequently, the combination of access to knowledge, social interaction at a distance and mediatization creates a site for the surreptitious infiltration of sociotechnical media systems into everyday life and self-formation in a way that, as Goffman (1959, 1983) suggested, involves social and cultural forms interacting with social metaprocesses.

POWERFUL MEDIA AND MEDIATED SELF-FORMATION

How is it that Goffman's ideas are experiencing a renaissance in the analysis of digital media at the same time as power-ful new media corporations appear to be capable of shaping everyday life, penetrating the very spaces in which Goffman's ideal of sociality is located (Hepp, 2020)? Is the capacity of participants in social encounters to constitute the situations they are part of, realize their social selves and shape their social worlds radically diminished by the reach of powerful media as part of the process of mediatization? Before discussing the implications of powerful media for the conditions in which social interaction, intersubjectivity, self-formation and civility might thrive, we should pause to reflect on Goffman's normative position.

Goffman's advocacy of the sociology of everyday life and his study of the interaction order as his core empirical project were clearly articulated. In contrast, his theoretical position remained implicit, leaving him open to criticism. In addition, his work was increasingly seen as out of touch and overtaken by more radical theoretical and political currents from the mid-1960s onwards. So much so that by 1970 this criticism had crystallized into a received view of Goffman's work in which he was lauded for his nuanced observations and interpretations of social interaction but also criticized for his lack of theory development (Gouldner, 1970). His normative position was also obscure, leaving him open to accusations of being a liberal apologist for mid-twentieth-century conservatism and a subjectivist who took little account of macro-sociological structures and processes.

However, Goffman's work on the asylum as a disciplinary institution (1961a) and his critique of the sociology of deviance through a focus on stigmatization (1963a) aligned him with the critical psychiatry movement, which identified medical interventions as forms of institutionalized social control. Also, Goffman's analysis of how participants in social encounters constitute the interaction order contrasts with the idea of individuals conforming to social norms and cultural values within a structure of authority. These insights run through his writings, providing alternatives to the social psychology of majority influence or conformity in favour of secondary adjustment and interactional strategies adopted in the face of influence and power. Goffman's work also reflects the liberal, reformist tradition of the Chicago School of Sociology, which aligns with progressive-era politics, within which Goffman inspired a critical work tradition. For example, Hochschild's (1983) participant observation study of Delta Airlines hostesses showed how self-presentation was appropriated as emotional labour by the requirements of the professional role. Consequently, emotional expressions were required to be controlled or 'feigned', in Goffman's (1959) terms, and actions directed to the service of pleasing the client and creating a conducive atmosphere for plane travel. Both Goffman's work on total institutions and social exclusion and Hochschild's work on emotional labour assert social interaction as a critical site of the struggle for autonomy in relation to systemic forms of social control in everyday life and social institutions.

Another perspective on the critical normative project of Goffman's work is reflected in his commentary on the increasing appropriation of everyday life in consumer society and the growing importance of consumption for identity (Lunt and Livingstone, 1992), which, when paired with the media, becomes a potent structuring constraint on social encounters (Hancock and Garner, 2015). For example, Goffman's analysis of gender portrayals in print advertising exposed a representation grounded in commercial realism presented through scenes from everyday life, dramatically scripted, inviting the audience to glimpse a world that had the potential to undermine the sense of what was genuine, authentic and autonomous (Hancock and Garner, 2015). Without going too far in aligning Goffman with critical theory, these examples demonstrate that he was questioning how consumer society and the media might change the context, resources and capacity for self-formation in significant ways.

Goffman was also writing against the grain of the sociology of his day, concerned about the loss of personal freedoms associated with the conformist political culture of the Cold War (Jaworski, 2022). However, a central theme in his work was that even in such unpromising circumstances people managed to sustain their social being, that portion of themselves that emphasized their collective identities, and through their practices constituted and sustained an interaction order that created a culture of civility and enabled self-formation even in the context of the powerful forces and dynamics of modernity (Giddens, 1990).

Initially, social media appeared to afford agency and sociality; for example, 'Facebook at its beginning epitomized the social networking model of enabling personal information sharing among users affiliated with each other through their educational background, geographic location, and so on' (Langlois and Elmer, 2019, p. 240). However, the development of platforms provided an infrastructure for mediated everyday life compounded by the development of increasingly sophisticated algorithms that guide choices and shape reactions (Langlois and Elmer, 2019; Plantin and Punathambekar, 2019). The influential work of van Dijck (2013) and Zuboff (2019) raises questions about digital and social media as means through which Big Tech potentially dominate individuals in their everyday lives. Through the deployment of datafication and algorithms, global corporations appear to have the capacity to frame choices, shape individual preferences and influence actions, thereby limiting the freedom and agency of subjects who are configured as consumers (van Dijck, 2013) susceptible to insidious behaviour modification techniques deployed by Big Tech corporations (Zuboff, 2019). Crucially, the capacity of individuals to act is enrolled as a source of value extraction, not least through the potential of digital media to reach into the self, resulting from the profusion of data generated by digital media and algorithmic processes of analysis that are both immediate and intimate in their relations to individuals: 'a power, less of persuasion than insinuation' (Zuboff, 2019, p. 279). Couldry and Mejias (2019) similarly characterize such processes of domination as the colonization of the self, which is seen as increasingly governed from the outside. These accounts challenge Goffman's faith in the potential of social interaction to break the frame, affording intersubjectivity, cooperation, recognition of common humanity and the formation of civility, social solidarity and interaction orders.

The self is consequently reconfigured as the product of exploitation by a production system, suggesting 'that the self has been rendered legible, docile, predictable, and tractable, subject to neo-behaviourist regimes of behaviour modification' (Brubaker, 2020, p. 795). Marwick (2013) captures the appropriation of public expressions of identity in a promotional culture extended to self-expression. Social control is treated as a form of governmentality, following Foucault's (1978) account of the constituting, defining, organizing and instrumentalizing of relations between people and self-formation. Although Foucault (1979) contrasted discursive power with disciplinary power, Marwick, in common with many interpretations in media studies, merges the two. Critical to this is the claim that neoliberalism propagates a concept of the self as a self-improving, self-sufficient individual (Marwick, 2013, p. 13).

Brubaker offers an alternative account of the self in the context of datafication that recognizes the neoliberal self as self-steering, self-actualizing, self-reflexive and entrepreneurial. However, Brubaker also follows the Mead/Goffman tradition in arguing that instead of working on already constituted selves from the outside, 'post-neoliberal selves enter into the constitution of the self, reshaping its internal workings, desires, rhythms, habits of attention, and modes of self-regulation' (2020, p. 794). Work on the self by Goffman, Foucault and Giddens provides alternative ways of 'understanding the transformation of the self by digital hyperconnectivity' (Brubaker, 2020, p. 795). Brubaker argues that digital media and cultures create new idioms for the self's construction, regulation and governance by both individuals and sociotechnical systems. He recognizes the expanded resources available to individuals through digital media in constituting, regulating and governing the self and, in parallel, the potential of sociotechnical systems to shape these dimensions of self-formation. The contrast between these two positions reframes the classical sociological question of the relationship between structure and agency. Do the freedoms that Goffman associated with self-formation through social interaction as constitutive practice still operate in digitally mediated contexts, or do sociotechnical systems now shape the processes of the self?

Burgess and Baym (2020, p. 1) argue that the openness of platforms and their integration with a culture of everyday life requires cultural analysis, in contrast to van Dijck and Poell's (2013) account of how the culture of connectivity as a social media logic shapes a set of market principles as a commonsense rationality cultivated in and by media. Burgess and Baym map the distinction between the features and affordances of the user interface and newsfeeds as the 'frontstage' in contrast to the 'backstage' technology, including software, algorithms and topic trends. They seek to put cultures of use on an equal footing with social media logics, allowing for how the latter are adopted and transformed through the actions of users. At the same time, they acknowledge the tendency of Twitter to become rationalized and dominated by commercial interests to the potential detriment of the capacity of users to shape the social media environment.

These arguments suggest that engagement with Goffman's account of self-formation as a constitutive practice in social interaction has some purchase in the study of self-regulation in the digital age and provides a way of interrogating claims about the insidious practices of powerful media while recognizing the spread of techniques of analysis associated with datafication.

INTERDISCIPLINARITY AND MEDIA SOCIOLOGY

What forms of interdisciplinarity are represented by the long-standing interest in Goffman's work in media and communication? First, there is the adoption in media research of Goffman's celebrated concepts that capture the nuances of social interactional dynamics and evoke a sensibility to sociological questions and themes. There are various orientations to these concepts; often, they are starting points for research, evocative ideas that resonate with the concerns and interests of media researchers. They have face validity even when transported from the study of copresent face-to-face communication to that of mediated social interaction. The development of digital communication technologies with interactional affordances makes Goffman's concepts more, not less, relevant to contemporary media and communication than in the past, when they were limited to studies of interpersonal communication and only problematically applied to mass communication (Thompson, 1995). As we have seen throughout this book, engagement with Goffman's work takes many forms, including abstraction, using his ideas as sensitizing concepts, treating them as having a life of their own separated from the context of his writing, but also often recognizing the theoretical commitments implicit in his writings, or pairing his ideas with theories from media research and sociology.

Sociology and media studies are separate disciplines with multiple points of overlap and interconnection, as illustrated here by the ways in which Goffman's sociology has been engaged with, adopted and adapted in media research. However, these are not, for the most part, examples of multidisciplinary endeavours in which concepts, theories and methods from two or more disciplines are equally drawn on in a research programme. Nor are they examples of nascent cross-disciplinary research programmes that constitute an emergent field of study, as in the case of science policy studies (Barry and Born, 2013). Complicating the picture is the fact that media and communication, in its disciplinary formation, emerged from a combination of sociology, social psychology, cultural and literary studies and political economy. Consequently, versions of sociological analysis and theory are dispersed throughout media studies.

However, the appropriation by media research of ideas from Goffman's writings can involve something other than an engagement with sociology as a discipline. Partly, there is something about the concepts Goffman coined and developed that enables them to travel well and lightly, to be transplanted, if not translated, into various disciplinary contexts. It is as if their meaning is exhausted by their ability to capture not the essence but a formulation of meaningful moments in social interaction, as detailed descriptions of forms of social practice and as sensitizing concepts for research. These concepts were gifts from Goffman; they offer media researchers detailed descriptions of elements of social practice loosely linked to sociological questions and theories. They are also an invitation to engage with sociological issues without having to take a stand on questions of sociological theory, since they do not commit the reader to a specific tradition or approach.

An engagement with Goffman's concepts and writings, then, brings analytic, normative and methodological resources that link media studies to questions of self-formation, power, social inequality, processes of individualization and the relation between structure and agency that are important counters to media-centrism (Waisbord, 2014). However, the relationship between sociology and media studies is asymmetrical: sociology is a source and resource for media scholars with relatively little take-up of media research in sociology. Waisbord (2014) argues that given its wide-ranging intellectual interests and its canon of work, sociology provides resources for a variety of disciplines as an exporter discipline. The borrowing of ideas from sociology by media studies has a complex history (Butsch, 2014); for example, the traditions of Chicago sociology as a multidisciplinary school provided an initial impetus for the study of the media. Since Goffman's writings were influenced by Chicago sociology, the relationship between his work and media studies has deep roots, as we have seen in the application of his ideas from the era of linear media to the digital age. However, sociology moved away from a direct engagement with the analysis of the media in the mid-twentieth century as the nascent discipline of media and communication emerged (Pooley and Katz, 2008). Waisbord illustrates this trend with the case of the initial interest in media framing by sociologists in the 1970s, followed by a profusion of frame analytic media studies that somewhat lost touch with the questions that sociologists ask concerning the relation between ideology and power, the dynamics of influence and strategic responses to media frames, and the balance between institutional power and bottom-up social movements.

The interplay between sociology and media studies is not a linear process, as illustrated by how frame analysis has reinvigorated interest in sociological questions such as the contestation of frames by social movements (Benford and Snow, 2000). As we have seen in this book, this story resonates with the manifold engagements of media researchers with Goffman's work, beginning with an interest in interpersonal communication and framing and subsequently reinvigorated by studies of digitally mediated social interaction and self-formation. However, if we are to engage the breadth of Goffman's writings in studying the mediation of interaction and the social implications of digital media, we have work to do, given that he did not explicitly theorize the sociological implications of the interaction order but demonstrated its relevance by exploring social interaction from a variety of sociological perspectives. How can we formulate an account of Goffman that goes beyond the patchwork of applications of his ideas within media and communication reviewed in this book? I will take some tentative steps in outlining the implications of Goffman's work for studying the social dimensions of digital media and society by taking the lead from a sociologist who has addressed this problem within sociology, Anthony Giddens (1984, 1990, 1991a).

STRUCTURATION AND THE RELATION BETWEEN THE INTERACTION ORDER AND SYSTEMIC FORMS OF SOCIAL INTEGRATION

While recognizing the limitations of taking a particular sociologist's work as a framework for thinking through the implications of Goffman's writing for digital media, in this case I think it is justified by the singular effort that Giddens has made throughout his career to see beyond the limitations of Goffman's theory development and the grounding of his work in the particularities of everyday life in the United States of the 1950s. Giddens views Goffman as making crucial contributions to an understanding of modern social life beyond his skilful depictions of the patterns and dynamics of social interactions, and seeks to integrate these insights into his own structuration theory (Giddens, 1984, p. xxiv) and theory of reflexive modernity (Giddens, 1991a; Scott, 2022). In this exercise, I am not by any means advocating Giddens's social theory as a framework for media studies, and recognize, for example, the importance of Bourdieu's (1977; 1990) critical stance on Goffman's work and his influence on media research (see Lunt, 2020). My aim is rather to gain insights into how the appropriation of Goffman's writings in media research might be integrated into the study of the social implications of digital media. Giddens seeks to fill in the theoretical gaps in Goffman's writing by embedding his account of the interaction order in a developed social theory that seeks to go beyond the dualism of structure and agency, offering an account of the relationship between social and system integration that links Goffman's analysis of the interaction order with social systems and structures in a process-oriented social theory. In his outline of structuration theory, Giddens (1984) engages Goffman's analysis of copresence in social encounters and the routines of social interactions, the analysis of material context, appearance and manner, and the importance of time and space in social encounters. In addition, Giddens recognizes Goffman's interactionist account of rules, roles, moral codes and social contexts in framing the routines of everyday social interaction.

In his outline of structuration theory, Giddens drew extensively on Goffman's analysis of social interaction, particularly the introduction to *Behaviour in Public Places* (Goffman, 1963b), arguing that while Goffman had provided a nuanced and sophisticated analysis of the dynamics and forms of social interaction, he had provided neither an explanation of how such forms originate nor an account of the implications of the interaction order for social systems. With his structuration theory, Giddens sought to explain how social structures create the conditions for the interaction order by providing rules, roles, moral codes and social contexts as both constraints on and resources for social interaction. Following rules and moral codes, playing out social roles and meeting the demands of social contexts, provide frameworks for social interaction as a form of social integration. Turning to how routines are implicated in social systems, Giddens focuses on their sedimentation as generalized behaviour patterns around which social systems are partly formed and sustained. He recognizes the symbolic interactionist aspects of Goffman's work, in particular that the apparent stability of institutions masks the dynamic underpinnings of systems integration in social interaction so that the routines of social interaction play a crucial role in social integration and reproduction. In addition, because everyday life extends into social organizations and systems, these patterns become part of the organization of social and cultural forms, institutions and public behaviour (Geuss, 2001). In his later work, Giddens argued that reflexive subjects orient their conduct to patterns of social behaviour, as these are reported in popular literature and self-help books, and which thereby contribute to establishing everyday regimes of social relations and shared understandings of appropriate social behaviour. However, this is now radically extended in the digital media environment and reflexive social institutions are increasingly oriented to the reflexive subject in commercial, NGO and governmental contexts. The question of social order is, therefore, best understood in terms of a mutual constitution in which existing social structures and social and cultural forms provide constraints and resources which afford the production of the interaction order, the routines of which contribute to systems integration through a process of structuration as reflexive social institutions react to patterns of social behaviour, creating a recurrent synergy between system and social integration.

There are two ways in which the adoptions of Goffman's writings in media studies I have presented in this book provide a perspective on his work that contrasts with the attempt to integrate micro-sociology in structuration theory and reflexive modernity theory. One brings out the symbolic interactionist aspects of Goffman's analysis of the interaction order, the other recognizes the various ways in which, through his engagement with different sociological perspectives, he provided suggestions about how interaction orders affect social orders beyond establishing widespread routines in social behaviour. These two aspects of Goffman's writing also help to explain the continuing relevance of his work in media studies beyond the value of his concepts in relation to the affordances of digital media and the spread of mediated interaction.

Goffman's analysis of the dynamics of engagements with rules, roles, moral codes and social contexts in social interaction recognizes their constraining nature. However, he argues that the orientation to these structuring principles is tempered by secondary adjustments and constitutive practices of social interaction rather than conformity. His work is full of examples of how rules range from formal to informal, how they are routinely contested, disobeyed, manipulated, and so on, so that it is the nature of the interaction order, a feature of its openness and creativity, to complicate the business of rule-following. Similarly, social roles are not merely played out in the drama of self-presentation but are routinely hedged with expressions of role distance. Moral codes, also – while sometimes routinely taken as guides to conduct, or as being driven by the desire to influence others' views of one's standing or qualities – reflect a view of ethical practice as arising during social encounters from synergies between the value to the individual of displaying and developing skilful participation in social practice which has value to them beyond the immediate situation and simultaneously contributes to the development of social practices as a form of virtue ethics (Macintyre, 1981).

Likewise, social contexts are partly given but also realized, modified and negotiated through the actions of participants. As Goffman's (1974) analysis of the personal front suggests, context, the definition of the situation and the framing of social encounters as ways of organizing experience are open to transformation and lamination in the course of interaction.

In addition, Goffman's writings, particularly in his engagement with various sociological perspectives, offer a range of ways, other than establishing routines of social behaviour, through which interaction orders potentially influence social coherence or systems integration. For example, his study of dramaturgy as a framework for understanding self-presentation as performance also draws attention to social encounters as proto-forms from which elements of professional theatre practices are derived through a process of rationalization and professionalization. Also, reflexive self-awareness of our performance of the self in everyday life is informed by theatrical traditions in a circuit of culture (Simmel, 1950). A further example is found in Goffman's account of ritual forms of organized experiences in social encounters, which are a significant source of politeness and civility, constituting an alignment between processes of mutual recognition and conditions of civil inattention that engender reverence towards others as rights-bearing individuals (Geuss, 2001). In his work on social order in public places, Goffman (1963b) points to interaction orders at the scale of events and gatherings in public places that directly contribute to social order beyond the level of face-to-face encounters. He emphasized the interactional dimensions of public order in the forms of 'situational propriety' in which individuals orient themselves to the demands of public order encompassing different degrees of involvement, the requirement to signal and sustain accessibility to others participating in the public gathering or event, and withholding attention to self and respecting others' space through a process of 'civil inattention' (Goffman, 1963b; Manning, 1992; Smith, 2022). These principles of the public interaction order surely provide resources for the analysis of conduct in online spaces (Burgess and Baym, 2020).

In his account of self-formation, Goffman also suggests a relationship between society and self in which participants are enrolled as 'self-regulating participants in social encounters' (Goffman, 1967, p. 44). This idea is reiterated in *Frame Analysis* (Goffman, 1974), in which social frames are understood as dependent on the actions and interactions of participants and are realized as constitutive practices (Rawls, 2012). Giddens (1991b) recognized the increasing salience of the media, albeit linear, in providing representations that frame rules, roles, moral codes and social contexts, supplementing the information available in the social and cultural forms of everyday life. Digital media radically extend access to information from multiple sources in addition to affording social interaction in mediated social encounters at a distance that reinforces these various and direct ways in which the interaction order contributes to social integration through order and disruption in the digital world.

FINAL THOUGHTS

This book has provided an analysis of the engagements with Goffman's writings in the study of media from the age of television to the current digital age. In response to his insistence on the paradigmatic status of face-to-face social interaction – in contrast to mediated interaction – in creating conditions in which individuals can realize their social

being and shape social encounters and broader social processes, the development of digital media technologies affords
forms of social interaction at a distance that overcome many
of Goffman's objections. Through manifold online social
relations participants can engage in social processes of self-
formation, individualization and rationalization, and engage
in the dynamics of relations between autonomy even in the
context of the reach of sociotechnical systems into everyday
life. Many of the forms and processes Goffman identified in
his analyses of face-to-face encounters are played out in digitally mediated contexts. They are, therefore, amenable to an
analysis of mediated interaction. An important effect of the
mediation of everything and of mediatization is the blurring
of boundaries between public and private, local and global,
regions of social life, expertise and everyday life. At the
same time as sociotechnical media systems spread into and
become powerful influences on everyday life and social practice, the opportunities of a media life afford unprecedented
connections, both private and public. In offering the potential to become part of a public at a distance and across scales,
they constitute a vastly extended environment, providing
resources for the organization of social interaction, self-formation and public connection. In addition, social interaction
constitutes the social media environment, extending the
analysis of the direct ways interaction orders contribute to
forms of system integration. For example, various forms of
the public appear in digital media environments, such as
affective publics (Papacharissi, 2015), social media publics
(Baym and boyd, 2012) and extended forms of public discussion and debate (Burgess and Baym, 2020).

The applications of Goffman's ideas in media studies
emphasize both the symbolic interactionist aspects of his
work – in which media environments offer the potential for
interpretation, contestation and negotiation – and various

orientations to rules, roles, moral codes and social contexts. In addition, the diverse impacts of the interaction order on system integration and social cohesion are recognizable in a media-saturated world. The first point looks beyond the following of rules and moral codes to reframing and negotiation as elements of constitutive practice. The second suggests that social interaction and participation contribute to system-level social integration beyond the effects of social reproduction through established, large-scale routines in social conduct.

In addition to these potential impacts of mediation and mediatization in framing the relationship between agency and structure, the social and cultural implications of the mediation of everything (Livingstone, 2009) and of mediatization (Lundby, 2014; Hjarvard, 2013; Hepp, 2020) mean that the opportunities offered to both users and sociotechnical media systems potentially exacerbate the dynamics of the 'experience of modernity' (Giddens, 1990, p. 139). Giddens provided a framework for understanding these dynamics in terms of adjusting to and coping with four dialectics that constitute experience in late modernity. These are: 'displacement and reembedding', 'intimacy and impersonality', 'expertise and reappropriation' and 'privatism and engagement' (1990, p. 140). In conclusion, I will suggest various ways the media are implicated in these dynamics, as illustrated by the appropriations of Goffman's ideas in media studies that have been reviewed throughout this book.

The mediation of social interaction (Chapter 3), the social implications of the interaction order (Chapter 4), and the role of mediated social interaction in the study of media phenomenology, media rituals and social media practice (Chapter 5), all play significant roles on both sides of the dynamics of modernity. The interpolation of media in these dynamics goes beyond providing resources and constraints for social interaction and explains the continuing relevance of Goffman's work in the digital age. Digital media environments intensify the 'intersection of estrangement and familiarity' in the manifold forms of sociality available online as participants gain ready access to multiple realities. Within digital media spaces, we confront 'the interaction of personal trust and impersonal ties' with varying dimensions of 'intimacy and trust', often within the same platform or application. Digital media have significant implications not only for 'the intersection of abstract systems and day-to-day knowledgeability' in the radical availability of expert commentary and shared experiences, but also for 'the intersection of pragmatic acceptance and activism' as sociotechnical systems develop increasingly sophisticated methods of shaping social behaviour while supporting new forms of life politics on a global scale, as in the case of environmentalism (Giddens, 1990, pp. 140–8).

The work in media and communication reviewed in this book suggests additional dialectics of the framing of experience in modernity alongside those identified by Giddens (1990). Firstly, the dynamic of self-formation in the context of powerful media creates a dialectic between individuals and sociotechnical systems in which resources for self-formation and reflexivity are available equally for self-monitoring and digitization. Secondly, the tension between an ethics of persuasion and an ethics grounded in participation in social practices (MacIntyre, 1981) creates a dynamic between the opportunities for people to connect and form associations beyond their locale and in contrast to the individualizing tendencies of media engagement. Thirdly, the expanded potential for self-expression is in tension with the imperatives of influence in social media contexts and the sustaining of sociality and significant social relationships. Finally, a radically expanded knowledge, both vernacular and expert, is in tension with the increased power of sociotechnical systems to manage and personalize access to information. In these ways, the affordances of digital media and the increasing sophistication and power of sociotechnical media systems create an expanded context for Goffman's depictions of the patterns and dynamics of social interaction at the core of everyday life.

REFERENCES

Abell, P. (1996) 'Rational choice theory and sociological theory', in Turner, B.S. (ed.) *The Blackwell Companion to Social Theory*. Oxford: Blackwell Publishing.

Altheide, D.L. and Snow, R.P. (1979) *Media Logic*. London: SAGE.

Anderson, N. (1923) *The Hobo: The Sociology of the Homeless Man*. Chicago: University of Chicago Press.

Andiloro, A. (2023) 'Understanding genre as atmospheric assemblage: The case of videogames', *Television & New Media*, 24(5), pp. 559–70.

Austin, J.L. (1962) *How to Do Things with Words*. Oxford: The Clarendon Press.

Ayaß, R. (2014) 'Using media as involvement shields', *Journal of Pragmatics*, 72, pp. 5–17.

Barry, A.B. and Born, G. (2013) *Interdisciplinarity: Reconfigurations of the Social and Natural Sciences*. London: Routledge.

Barthes, R. (1972) *Critical Essays*. Evanston: Northwestern University Press.

Bateson, G. (1973) *Steps to an Ecology of Mind*. London: Fontana.

Bausinger, H. (1984) 'Media, technology and daily life', *Media, Culture & Society*, 6(4), pp. 343–51.

Baym, N.K. (2010) *Personal Connections in the Digital Age*. Cambridge: Polity Press.

Baym, N.K. (2015) *Personal Connections in the Digital Age*. 2nd edn. Cambridge: Polity Press.

Baym, N.K. and boyd, d. (2012) 'Socially mediated publicness: An introduction', *Journal of Broadcasting & Electronic Media*, 56(3), pp. 320–9.

Beck, U. and Beck-Gernsheim, E. (2002) *Individualization: Institutionalized Individualism and its Social and Political Consequences*. London: SAGE.

Bell, D. (1976) *The Coming of Post-Industrial Society: A Venture in Social Forecasting*. New York: Basic Books.

Benford, R.D. (2013) 'Social movements and the dramatic framing of social reality', in Edgley, C. (ed.) *The Drama of Social Life*. London: Routledge.

Benford, R.D. and Snow, D.A. (2000) 'Framing processes and social movements: An overview and assessment', *Annual Review of Sociology*, 26(1), pp. 611–39.

Berger, J. (1972) *Ways of Seeing*. Harmondsworth: Penguin Books.

Berger, P.L. and Luckmann, T. (1966) *The Social Construction of Reality: A Treatise in the Sociology of Knowledge*, Harmondsworth: Penguin Books.

Blackwell, C., Birnholtz, J. and Abbott, C. (2015) 'Seeing and being seen: Co-situation and impression formation using Grindr, a location-aware gay dating app', *New Media & Society*, 17(7), pp. 1117–36.

Blumer, H. (1992 [1969]) *Symbolic Interactionism: Perspective and Method*. 3rd edn. Berkeley: University of California Press.

Boltanski, L. and Chiapello, E. (2006) *The New Spirit of Capitalism*. London: Verso.

Bourdieu, P. (1977) *Outline of a Theory of Practice*. Cambridge: Cambridge University Press.

Bourdieu, P. (1990) *The Logic of Practice*. Stanford, CA: Stanford University Press.

Bourdieu, P. (1991) *Language and Symbolic Power*. Cambridge: Polity Press.

boyd, d. (2006) 'Friends, friendsters, and top 8: Writing community into being on social network sites', *First Monday*, 11(12).

boyd, d. and Ellison, N.B. (2007) 'Social network sites: Definition, history, and scholarship', *Journal of Computer-Mediated Communication*, 13(1), pp. 210–30.

Boyd, M.S. (2014) '(New) participatory framework on YouTube? Commenter interaction in US political speeches', *Journal of Pragmatics*, 72, pp. 46–58.

Brand, G. and Scannell, P. (1991) 'Talk, identity and performance', in Scannell, P. (ed.) *Broadcast Talk*. London: SAGE.

Bräuchler, B. and Postill, J. (eds.) (2010) *Theorising Media and Practice*. Oxford and New York: Berghahn Books.

Brown, P. and Levinson, S.C. (1987) *Politeness: Some Universals in Language Usage*. Cambridge: Cambridge University Press.

Brubaker, R. (2020) 'Digital hyperconnectivity and the self', *Theory and Society*, 49(5–6), pp. 771–801.

Bucher, T. and Helmond, A. (2018) 'The affordances of social media platforms', in Burgess, J., Marwick, A. and Poell, T. (eds.) *The SAGE Handbook of Social Media*. London: SAGE.

Bullingham, L. and Vasconcelos, A.C. (2013) 'The presentation of self in the online world: Goffman and the study of online identities', *Journal of Information Science*, 39(1), pp. 101–12.

Bulmer, M. (1984) *The Chicago School of Sociology*. Chicago: University of Chicago Press.

Burgess, J. and Baym, N.K. (2020) *Twitter: A Biography*. New York: New York University Press.

Burgess, J., Marwick, A.E. and Poell, T. (2018) *The Sage Handbook of Social Media*. London: SAGE.

Butler, J. (1988) 'Performative acts and gender constitution: An essay in phenomenology and feminist theory', *Theatre Journal*, 40(4).

Butler, J. (1990) *Gender Trouble*. New York: Routledge.

Butsch, R. (2014) 'Agency, social interaction, and audience studies', in Waisbord, S. (ed.) *Media Sociology: A Reappraisal*. Cambridge: Polity Press.

Calhoun, C.J. (2007) *Sociology in America*. Chicago: University of Chicago Press.

Castells, M. (2015) *Networks of Outrage and Hope: Social Movements in the Internet Age*. Cambridge: Polity Press.

Chambers, D. (2013) *Social Media and Personal Relationships*. Basingstoke: Palgrave Macmillan.

Chen, S. and Lunt, P. (2021) *Chinese Social Media: Face, Sociality and Civility*. Bingley: Emerald Publishing.

Chester, A. and Bretherton, D. (2007) 'Impression management and identity online', in Joinson, A., McKenna, K.Y.A., Postmes, T. and Reips, U.-D. (eds.) *The Oxford Handbook of Internet Psychology*. Oxford: Oxford University Press.

Chouliaraki, L. (2006) *The Spectatorship of Suffering*. London: SAGE.

Clegg, S.R. and Haugaard, M. (2009) *The SAGE Handbook of Power*. London: SAGE.

Cohen, É.A. (1953) *Human Behavior in the Concentration Camp*. New York: W.W. Norton.

Collins, R. (1994) *Four Sociological Traditions* (Revised and expanded edition of *Three Sociological Traditions: Selected Readings*). Oxford: Oxford University Press.

Collins, R. (2004) *Interaction Ritual Chains*. Princeton, NJ: Princeton University Press.

Cooley, C.H. (1922) *Human Nature and the Social Order*. New York: C. Scribner's Sons.

Corner, J. (1991) 'The interview as social encounter', in Scannell, P. (ed.) *Broadcast Talk*. London: SAGE.

Couldry, N. (2002) *Media Rituals: A Critical Approach*. London: Routledge.

Couldry, N. (2004) 'Theorising media as practice', *Social Semiotics*, 14(2), pp. 115–32.

Couldry, N. (2013) *Media, Society, World: Social Theory and Digital Media Practice*. Oxford: Wiley.

Couldry, N. and Hepp, A. (2013) 'Conceptualising mediatization: Contexts, traditions, arguments', *Communication Theory*, 23, pp. 191–202.

Couldry, N. and Hepp, A. (2017) *The Mediated Construction of Reality*. Cambridge: Polity Press.

Couldry, N. and Mejias, U. (2019) *The Costs of Connection: How Data Is*

Colonizing Human Life and Appropriating It for Capitalism. Stanford: Stanford University Press.

Crossley, N. (1996) *Intersubjectivity: The Fabric of Social Becoming.* London: SAGE.

Daniels, J., Gregory, K. and McMillan, C. (2017) *Digital Sociologies.* Bristol: Policy Press.

Dayan, D. and Katz, E. (1992) *Media Events: The Live Broadcasting of History.* Cambridge, MA: Harvard University Press.

de Certeau, M. (1984) *The Practice of Everyday Life.* Berkeley: University of California Press.

Dencik, L. (2018) 'Surveillance realism and the politics of imagination: Is there no alternative?', *Krisis*, 38(1), pp. 31–43.

Deuze, M. (2012) *Media Life.* Cambridge: Polity Press.

Ditchfield, H. and Lunt, P. (2020) 'Re-configuring synchronicity and sequentiality in online interaction: Multicommunication on Facebook messenger', in Kaun, A., Pentzold, C. and Lohmeier, C. (eds.) *Making Time for Digital Lives: Beyond Chronotopia.* London: Rowman & Littlefield.

Dominick, J.R. (1999) 'Who do you think you are? Personal home pages and self-presentation on the World Wide Web', *Journalism & Mass Communication Quarterly*, 76(4), pp. 646–58.

Donath, J. (2014) *The Social Machine: Designs for Living Online.* Cambridge, MA: MIT Press.

Duneier, M., Kasinitz, P. and Murphy, A. (2014) *The Urban Ethnography Reader.* New York: Oxford University Press.

Durkheim, É. (1984 [1893]) *The Division of Labour in Society.* London, Macmillan.

Durkheim, É. (1995 [1912]) *The Elementary Forms of the Religious Life.* New York: Free Press.

Durkheim, É. (2005 [1914]) 'The dualism of human nature and its social conditions', *Durkheimian Studies*, 11(1), pp. 35–45.

Eberle, T.S. (2012) 'Phenomenological life-world analysis and ethnomethodology's program', *Human Studies*, 35(2), pp. 279–304.

Eisenlauer, V. (2014) 'Facebook as a third author: (Semi-)automated participation framework in social network sites', *Journal of Pragmatics*, 72, pp. 73–85.

Elias, N. (2000) *The Civilizing Process.* Oxford: Wiley-Blackwell.

Ellison, N.R., Heino, R. and Gibbs, J. (2006) 'Managing impressions online: Self-presentation processes in the online dating environment', *Journal of Computer-Mediated Communication*, 11(2), pp. 415–41.

Entman, R.M. (1993) 'Framing: Toward clarification of a fractured paradigm', *Journal of Communication*, 43(4), pp. 51–8.

Floridi, L. (2014) *The Fourth Revolution: How the Infosphere Is Reshaping Human Reality*. Oxford: Oxford University Press.

Foucault, M. (1964) *Madness and Civilization: A History of Insanity in the Age of Reason*. New York: Vintage Books.

Foucault, M. (1978) *The History of Sexuality*. New York: Vintage Books.

Foucault, M. (1979) *Discipline and Punish: The Birth of the Prison*. New York: Vintage Books.

Foucault, M. (1990) *The History of Sexuality: An Introduction*. New York: Knopf.

Frobenius, M. (2014) 'Audience design in monologues: How vloggers involve their viewers', *Journal of Pragmatics*, 72, pp. 59–72.

Gaddis, J.L. (2006) *The Cold War*. New York: Penguin Books.

Gamson, W.A. (1985) 'Goffman's legacy to political sociology', *Theory and Society*, 14(5), pp. 605–22.

Gamson, W.A. (1995) 'Hiroshima, the Holocaust, and the politics of exclusion: 1994 Presidential Address', *American Sociological Review*, 60(1), pp. 1–20.

Gamson, W.A., Croteau, D., Hoynes, W. and Sasson, T. (1992) 'Media images and the social construction of reality', *Annual Review of Sociology*, 18(1), pp. 373–93.

Gamson, W.A. and Modigliani, A. (1989) 'Media discourse and public opinion on nuclear power: A constructionist approach', *The American Journal of Sociology*, 95(1), pp. 1–37.

Garfinkel, H. (1967) *Studies in Ethnomethodology*. Englewood Cliffs, NJ: Prentice Hall.

Gergen, K. (1991) *The Saturated Self: Dilemmas of Identity in Contemporary Life*. New York: Basic Books.

Geuss, R. (2001) *Public Goods, Private Goods*. Princeton, NJ: Princeton University Press, Princeton.

Gibbs, J.L., Ellison, N.B. and Heino, R.D. (2006) 'Self-presentation in online personals', *Communication Research*, 33(2), pp. 152–77.

Gibson, J.J. (2015) *The Ecological Approach to Visual Perception*. 1st edn. London: Psychology Press.

Giddens, A. (1979) *Central Problems in Social Theory*. London: Bloomsbury.

Giddens, A. (1984) *The Constitution of Society: Outline of the Theory of Structuration*. Oakland: University of California Press.

Giddens, A. (1990) *The Consequences of Modernity*. Cambridge: Polity Press.

Giddens, A. (1991a) *Modernity and Self-Identity*. Cambridge: Polity Press.

Giddens, A. (1991b) 'Erving Goffman as a systematic social theorist', in *Social Theory and Modern Sociology*. Cambridge: Polity Press.

Giddens, A. (2009) 'On rereading *The Presentation of Self*: Some reflections', *Social Psychology Quarterly*, 72(4), pp. 290–5.

Gitlin, T. (1987) *The Sixties: Years of Hope, Days of Rage*. New York: Bantam Books.

Goffman, E. (1955) 'On face-work', *Psychiatry*, 18(3), pp. 213–31.

Goffman, E. (1956) 'The nature of deference and demeanor', *American Anthropologist*, 58(3), pp. 473–502.

Goffman, E. (1959) *The Presentation of Self in Everyday Life*. New York: Doubleday.

Goffman, E. (1961a) *Asylums: Essays on the Condition of the Social Situation of Mental Patients and Other Inmates*. New York: Anchor Books.

Goffman, E. (1961b) *Encounters*. Indianapolis, IN: Bobbs-Merrill.

Goffman, E. (1963a) *Stigma: Notes on the Management of Spoiled Identity*. Englewood Cliffs, NJ: Prentice Hall.

Goffman, E. (1963b) *Behavior in Public Places: Notes on the Social Organization of Gatherings*. New York: The Free Press of Glencoe.

Goffman, E. (1967) *Interaction Ritual: Essays in Face-to-face Behavior*. Chicago: Aldine.

Goffman, E. (1969) *Strategic Interaction*. Oxford: Basil Blackwell.

Goffman, E. (1974) *Frame Analysis: An Essay on the Organization of Experience*. Harmondsworth: Penguin Books.

Goffman, E. (1979) *Gender Advertisements*. New York and London: Harper & Row.

Goffman, E. (1981) *Forms of Talk*. Philadelphia: University of Pennsylvania Press.

Goffman, E. (1983) 'The interaction order: American Sociological Association, 1982 Presidential Address', *American Sociological Review*, 48(1), pp. 1–17.

Goffman, E. (2022 [1953]) 'Communication conduct in an island community', PhD, University of Chicago, at https://directory.doabooks.org/handle/20.500.12854/94926.

Gouldner, A.W. (1970) *The Coming Crisis of Western Sociology*. New York: Basic Books.

Graham, S.L. and Hardaker, C. (2017) '(Im)politeness in digital communication', in Culpeper, J., Haugh, M. and Kádár, D.Z. (eds.) *The Palgrave Handbook of Linguistic (Im)politeness*. London: Palgrave Macmillan.

Granovetter, M.S. (1973) 'The strength of weak ties', *American Journal of Sociology*, 78(6), pp. 1360–80.

Habermas, J. (1984) *The Theory of Communicative Action*. London: Heinemann.

Habermas, J. (1991) *The Structural Transformation of the Public Sphere*. Cambridge, MA: MIT Press.

Hancock, B.H. and Garner, R. (2015) 'Erving Goffman: Theorizing the self in the age of advanced consumer capitalism', *Journal for the Theory of Social Behaviour*, 45(2), pp. 163–87.

Hannem, S. (2022) 'Stigma', in Jacobsen, M.H. and Smith, G. (eds.) *The Routledge International Handbook of Goffman Studies*. London: Routledge.

Hepp, A. (2020) *Deep Mediatization*. London: Routledge.

Hill, A., Weibull, L. and Nilsson, A. (2005) *Audiences and Factual and Reality Television in Sweden*. Jonkoping: Hogskolan i Jonkoping.

Hjarvard, S. (2013) *The Mediatization of Culture and Society*. London: Routledge.

Hochschild, A.R. (1983) *The Managed Heart: Commercialization of Human Feeling*. Berkeley: University of California Press.

Hogan, B. (2010) 'The presentation of self in the age of social media: Distinguishing performances and exhibitions online', *Bulletin of Science, Technology & Society*, 30(6), pp. 377–86.

Holquist, M., Emerson, C. and Bakhtin, M.M. (1981) *The Dialogic Imagination: Four Essays*. Austin: University of Texas Press.

Hsieh, Y.P. (2012) 'Online social networking skills: The social affordances approach to digital inequality', *First Monday*, 17(4).

Hutchby, I. (2001) 'Technologies, Texts and Affordances', *Sociology*, 35(2), pp. 441–56.

Hutchby, I. (2014) 'Communicative affordances and participation frameworks in mediated interaction', *Journal of Pragmatics*, 72, pp. 86–9.

Isin, E.F. (2008) 'Theorizing acts of citizenship', in Isin, E.F. and Nielsen, G.M. (eds.) *Acts of Citizenship*. London: Palgrave Macmillan.

Isin, E.F. and Ruppert, E. (2020) *Being Digital Citizens*. 2nd edn. London and New York: Rowman & Littlefield.

Ivana, G.I. (2014) *Authenticity on Facebook: Between Exposure and Self-representation*. IN3 Working paper series. Barcelona: Internet Interdisciplinary Institute (IN3), at https://eprints.gla.ac.uk/183173/1/183173.pdf.

Ivana, G.I. (2016) 'Present contemporaries and absent consociates: Rethinking Schütz's "We relation" beyond copresence', *Human Studies*, 39(4), pp. 513–31.

Jacobsen, M.H. (2010) *The Contemporary Goffman*. London: Routledge.

Jacobsen, M.H. and Kristiansen, S. (2010) 'Labelling Goffman: The presentation and appropriation of Erving Goffman in academic life', in Jacobsen, M.H. (ed.) *The Contemporary Goffman*. London: Routledge.

Jacobsen, M.H. and Smith, G. (eds.) (2022) *The Routledge International Handbook of Goffman Studies*. London: Routledge.

James, W. (1950 [1890]) *The Principles of Psychology*. Mineola, NY: Dover Publications.

Jaworski, G.D. (2022) 'Strategic interaction', in Jacobsen, M.H. and Smith, G. (eds.) *The Routledge International Handbook of Goffman Studies*. London: Routledge.

Katz, J.E. and Aakhus, M. (2002) *Perpetual Contact: Mobile Communications, Private Talk, Public Performance*. Cambridge: Cambridge University Press.

Katz, J.E. and Rice, R.E. (2002) *Social Consequences of Internet Use: Access, Involvement, and Interaction*. Cambridge, MA: MIT Press.

Kesey, K. (1962) *One Flew Over the Cuckoo's Nest*. Harmondsworth: Penguin Books.

Kogon, E. (1950) *The Theory and Practice of Hell: The German*

Concentration Camps and the System Behind Them. New York: Farrar, Strauss.

Kraut, R., Patterson, M., Lundmark, V., Kiesler, S., Mukopadhyay, T. and Scherlis, W. (1998) 'Internet paradox', *The American Psychologist*, 53(9), pp. 1017–31.

Kress, G. (2010) *Multimodality: A Social Semiotic Approach to Contemporary Communication.* London: Routledge.

Krotz, F. (2007) 'The meta-process of "mediatization" as a conceptual frame', *Global Media and Communication*, 3(3), pp. 256–60.

Laclau, E. (2005) *On Populist Reason.* New York: Verso.

Laing, R.D. (1960) *The Divided Self.* London: Tavistock Publications.

Langlois, G. and Elmer, G. (2019) 'Impersonal subjectivation from platforms to infrastructures', *Media, Culture & Society*, 41(2), pp. 236–51.

Leary, M.R. and Kowalski, R.M. (1990) 'Impression management', *Psychological Bulletin*, 107(1), pp. 34–47.

Lee, K.M. (2004) 'Presence, explicated', *Communication Theory*, 14(1), pp. 27–50.

Licoppe, C. (2004) '"Connected" presence: The emergence of a new repertoire for managing social relationships in a changing communication technoscape', *Environment and Planning D, Society & Space*, 22(1), pp. 135–56.

Lim, S.S. and Basnyat, I. (2016) 'Face and online social networking', in Lim, S.S. and Soriano, C. (eds.) *Asian Perspectives on Digital Culture: Emerging Phenomena, Enduring Concepts.* London: Routledge.

Ling, R.S. (2008) *New Tech, New Ties.* Cambridge, MA: MIT Press.

Livingstone, S. (2004) 'The challenge of changing audiences', *European Journal of Communication*, 19(1), pp. 75–86.

Livingstone, S. (2005) *Audiences and Publics: When Cultural Engagement Matters for the Public Sphere.* Bristol: Intellect.

Livingstone, S. (2008) 'Taking risky opportunities in youthful content creation: Teenagers' use of social networking sites for intimacy, privacy and self-expression', *New Media & Society*, 10(3), pp. 393–411.

Livingstone, S. (2009) 'On the mediation of everything', *Journal of Communication*, 59, pp. 1–18.

Livingstone, S. and Lunt, P.K. (1994) *Talk on Television.* London: Routledge.

Lundby, K. (2014) *Mediatization of Communication.* Berlin: De Gruyter.

Lunt, P. (2019) 'The performance of power and citizenship: David Cameron meets the people', *International Journal of Cultural Studies*, 22(5), pp. 678–90.

Lunt, P. (2020) 'Beyond Bourdieu: The interactionist foundations of media practice theory', *International Journal of Communication*, 14, pp. 2946–63.

Lunt, P. (2022) 'The reception of Goffman's work in media studies', in Jacobsen, M.H. and Smith, G. (eds.) *The Routledge International Handbook of Goffman Studies*. London: Routledge.

Lunt, P. and Livingstone, S. (1992) *Mass Consumption and Personal Identity: Everyday Economic Experience*. Philadelphia, PA: Open University Press.

MacIntyre, A. (1981) *After Virtue: A Study in Moral Theory*. Notre Dame, IN: University of Notre Dame Press.

MacKenzie, D.A. and Wajcman, J. (1988) *The Social Shaping of Technology*. Milton Keynes: Open University Press.

McLuhan, M. (1964) *Understanding Media: The Extensions of Man*. New York: McGraw-Hill.

Madianou, M. (2016) 'Ambient co-presence: Transnational family practices in polymedia environments', *Global Networks*, 16(2), pp. 183–201.

Madianou, M. and Miller, D. (2012) *Migration and New Media*. London: Routledge.

Manning, P. (1992) *Erving Goffman and Modern Sociology*. Cambridge: Polity Press.

Markham, T. and Rodgers, S. (eds.) (2017) *Conditions of Mediation: Phenomenological Perspectives on Media*. New York: Peter Lang.

Marwick, A.E. (2013) *Status Update: Celebrity, Publicity, and Branding in the Social Media Age*. New Haven, CT: Yale University Press.

Marwick, A.E. (2020) 'Media studies and the pitfalls of publicity', *Television & New Media*, 21(6), pp. 608–15.

Marwick, A.E. and boyd, d. (2011) 'I tweet honestly, I tweet passionately: Twitter users, context collapse, and the imagined audience', *New Media & Society*, 13(1), pp. 114–33.

Mead, G.H. (1934) *Mind, Self and Society from the Standpoint of a Social Behaviorist*. Chicago: University of Chicago Press.

Mendelson, A.L. and Papacharissi, Z. (2010) 'Look at us: Collective narcissism in college student Facebook photo galleries', in *A Networked Self: Identity, Community, and Culture on Social Network Sites*. New York: Routledge.

Merton, R.K. (1957) *Social Theory and Social Structure*. Glencoe, IL: The Free Press.

Meyrowitz, J. (1985) *No Sense of Place: The Impact of Electronic Media on Social Behavior*. New York: Oxford University Press.

Miller, D. (2011) *Tales from Facebook*. Cambridge: Polity Press.

Miller, H. (1995) 'The presentation of self in electronic life: Goffman on the internet'. Paper presented at Embodied Knowledge and Virtual Space Conference, Goldsmiths College, University of London, June, at www.dourish.com/classes/ics234cw04/miller2.pdf.

Mills, C.W. (1967) *The Sociological Imagination*. Oxford: Oxford University Press.

Misak, C. (2013) *The American Pragmatists*. Oxford: Oxford University Press.

Mische, A. (2011) 'Relational sociology, culture, and agency', in Scott, J. and Carrington, P.J. (eds.) *The SAGE Handbook of Social Network Analysis*. London: SAGE.

Moores, S. (2011) 'That familiarity with the world born of habit: A phenomenological approach to the study of media uses in daily living', *Interactions*, 1(3), pp. 301–12.

Mouffe, C. (1993) *Return of the Political*. London: Verso.

Mulyana, N. and Qomariana, Y. (2023) 'Face maintenance rituals and communication strategies used in Puja Astawa's YouTube videos', *Lensa*, 13(1), pp. 30–48.

Nagy, P. and Neff, G. (2015) 'Imagined affordance: Reconstructing a keyword for communication theory', *Social Media and Society*, 1(2).

Nie, N.H. (2001) 'Sociability, interpersonal relations, and the internet', *The American Behavioral Scientist*, 45(3), pp. 420–35.

Norman, D.A. (1988) *The Psychology of Everyday Things*. New York: Basic Books.

Ozansoy Çadırcı, T. and Sağkaya Güngör, A. (2016) 'Love my selfie: Selfies in managing impressions on social networks', *Journal of Marketing Communications*, 25(3), pp. 268–87.

Papacharissi, Z. (2002) 'The presentation of self in virtual life:

Characteristics of personal home pages', *Journalism & Mass Communication Quarterly*, 79(3), pp. 643–60.

Papacharissi, Z. (ed.) (2010) *A Networked Self: Identity, Community, and Culture on Social Network Sites*. New York: Routledge.

Papacharissi, Z. (2015) *Affective Publics: Sentiment, Technology, and Politics*. Oxford: Oxford University Press.

Park, R.E., Burgess, E.W. and McKenzie, R.D. (1967 [1925]) *The City*. Chicago: University of Chicago Press.

Parsons, T. (1937) *The Structure of Social Action*. New York: McGraw-Hill.

Parsons, T. (1951) *The Social System*. Glencoe, IL: Free Press.

Peirce, C.S. (2012) *Philosophical Writings of Peirce*. Mineola, NY: Dover Publications.

Persson, A. (2022) 'Frame analysis', in Jacobsen, M.H. and Smith, G. (eds.) *The Routledge International Handbook of Goffman Studies*. London: Routledge.

Peters, J.D. (1999) *Speaking into the Air*. Chicago: University of Chicago Press.

Peters, J.D. and Simonson, P. (2004) *Mass Communication and American Social Thought*. Lanham, MD: Rowman & Littlefield.

Pinch, T. (2010) 'The invisible technologies of Goffman's sociology: From the merry-go-round to the internet', *Technology and Culture*, 51(2), pp. 409–24.

Plantin, J. and Punathambekar, A. (2019) 'Digital media infrastructures: Pipes, platforms, and politics', *Media, Culture & Society*, 41(2), pp. 163–74.

Plummer, K. (2000) 'Symbolic interaction in the twentieth century', in Turner, B.S. (ed.) *The Blackwell Companion to Social Theory*. Oxford: Blackwell.

Pooley, J. and Katz, E. (2008) 'Further notes on why American sociology abandoned mass communication research', *Journal of Communication*, 58(4), pp. 767–86.

Poster, M. (1995) *The Second Media Age*. Cambridge: Polity Press.

Putnam, R.D. (2020) *Bowling Alone*. 20th anniversary edn. New York: Simon & Schuster.

Rawls, A.W. (1987) 'The interaction order sui generis: Goffman's contribution to social theory', *Sociological Theory*, 5(2), pp. 136–49.

Rawls, A.W. (2011) 'Wittgenstein, Durkheim, Garfinkel and Winch: Constitutive orders of sensemaking', *Journal for the Theory of Social Behaviour*, 41(4), pp. 396–418.

Rawls, A.W. (2012) 'Durkheim's theory of modernity: Self-regulating practices as constitutive orders of social and moral facts', *Journal of Classical Sociology*, 12(3–4), pp. 479–512.

Rawls, A.W. (2022) 'Situating Goffman's "interaction orders" in Durkheim's social fact lineage. Grounding an alternate sociology of modernity in heightened awareness of interaction', *Etnografia e Ricerca Qualitativa*, 15(1), pp. 27–62.

Robinson, L. (2007) 'The cyberself: The self-ing project goes online, symbolic interaction in the digital age', *New Media & Society*, 9(1), pp. 93–110.

Rock, P. (1979) *The Making of Symbolic Interactionism*. London: Macmillan.

Rogers, M. (1977) 'Goffman on power', *The American Sociologist*, 12(2), pp. 88–95.

Rose, N.S. (1999) *Governing the Soul: The Shaping of the Private Self*. London: Free Association Books.

Rosenberg, M.M. (2022) 'The interaction order', in Jacobsen, M.H. and Smith, G. (eds.) *The Routledge International Handbook of Goffman Studies*. London: Routledge.

Rothenbuhler, E.W. (1998) *Ritual Communication*. Thousand Oaks, CA: SAGE.

Sartre, J.-P. (1956) *Being and Nothingness: An Essay on Phenomenological Ontology*. New York: Philosophical Library.

Scannell, P. (ed.) (1991) *Broadcast Talk*. London: SAGE.

Scannell, P. (1996) *Radio, Television and Modern Life*. Oxford: Wiley-Blackwell.

Scannell, P. (2014) *Television and the Meaning of 'Live': An Enquiry into the Human Situation*. Cambridge: Polity Press.

Scannell, P. and Cardiff, D. (1991) *A Social History of British Broadcasting*. Oxford: Blackwell.

Schelling, T.C. (1979 [1960]) *The Strategy of Conflict*. Cambridge, MA: Harvard University Press.

Schlenker, B.R. (2012) 'Self-presentation', in Leary, M.R. and Tangney, J.P. (eds.) *Handbook of Self and Identity*. New York: Guilford Press.

Schlenker, B.R. and Weigold, M.F. (1992) 'Interpersonal processes involving impression regulation and management', *Annual Review of Psychology*, 43(1), pp. 133–68.

Schröder, K. (2017) 'Towards the "audiencization" of mediatization research? Audience dynamics as co-constitutive of mediatization processes', in Driessens, O., Bolin, G., Hepp, A. and Hjarvard, S. (eds.) *Dynamics of Mediatization*. Cham: Springer International.

Schröder, R. (2010) *Being There Together: Social Interaction in Virtual Environments*. Oxford: Oxford University Press.

Schultze, U. and Brooks, J.A.M. (2019) 'An interactional view of social presence: Making the virtual other "real"', *Information Systems Journal*, 29(3), pp. 707–37.

Schutz, A. (1967) *The Phenomenology of the Social World*. Evanston, IL: Northwestern University Press.

Scott, J. (2022) 'Goffman and Giddens', in Jacobsen, M.H. and Smith, G. (eds.) *The Routledge International Handbook of Goffman Studies*. London: Routledge.

Sidnell, J. (2022) 'Reframing "footing"', in Jacobsen, M.H. and Smith, G. (eds.) *The Routledge International Handbook of Goffman Studies*. London: Routledge.

Siles, I. (2017) *Networked Selves: Trajectories of Blogging in the United States and France*. New York: Peter Lang.

Simmel, G. (1950) *The Sociology of Georg Simmel*. Glencoe, IL: The Free Press.

Simon, H.A. (1982) *Models of Bounded Rationality*. Cambridge, MA: MIT Press.

Smith, G. (2006) *Erving Goffman*. London: Taylor and Francis.

Smith, G. (2010) 'Reconsidering gender advertisements: Performativity, framing and display', in Jacobsen, M.H. (ed.) *The Contemporary Goffman*. London: Routledge.

Smith, R.J. (2022) 'Interaction in public places', in Jacobsen, M.H. and Smith, G. (eds.) *The Routledge International Handbook of Goffman Studies*. London: Routledge.

Sobchack, V. (1992) *The Address of the Eye: A Phenomenology of Film Experience*. Princeton, NJ: Princeton University Press.

Stryker, S. and Burke, P.J. (2000) 'The past, present, and future of an identity theory', *Social Psychology Quarterly*, 63(4), pp. 284–97.

Sylvester, S. (2019) 'The theatre of the selfie: Fictive practices of the Instagram artist', *Body, Space & Technology Journal*, 18(1), pp. 61–107.

Szasz, T. (1961) *The Myth of Mental Illness: Foundations of a Theory of Personal Conduct*. New York: Harper & Row.

Taylor, D. and Altman, I. (1987) 'Communication in interpersonal relationships: Social penetration processes', *SAGE Annual Reviews of Communications Research*, 14, p. 257.

Thompson, J.B. (1995) *The Media and Modernity: A Social Theory of the Media*. Cambridge: Polity Press.

Thompson, J.B. (2018) 'Mediated interaction in the digital age', *Matrizes*, 12(3), pp. 17–44.

Torpey, J. (2020) 'A sociological agenda for the tech age', *Theory and Society*, 49(5–6), pp. 749–69.

Turkle, S. (1996) *Life on the Screen: Identity in the Age of the Internet*. London: Weidenfeld & Nicholson.

Turner, V.W. (1977) *The Ritual Process: Structure and Anti-Structure*. Ithaca, NY: Cornell University Press.

Turner, V.W. (1982) *From Ritual to Theatre: The Human Seriousness of Play*. New York: PAJ Publications.

Tyler, I. (2020) *Stigma: The Machinery of Inequality*. London: Zed Books.

Uski, S. and Lampinen, A. (2014) 'Social norms and self-presentation on social network sites: Profile work in action', *New Media & Society*, 18(3), pp. 447–64.

van Dijck, J. (2013) '"You have one identity": Performing the self on Facebook and LinkedIn', *Media, Culture & Society*, 35(2), pp. 199–215.

van Dijck, J. and Poell, T. (2013) 'Understanding social media logic', *Media and Communication*, 1(1), pp. 2–14.

Waisbord, S. (2014) *Media Sociology: A Reappraisal*. Oxford: Wiley.

Walther, J.B. (1996) 'Computer-mediated communication', *Communication Research*, 23(1), pp. 3–43.

Walther, J.B. and Burgoon, J.K. (1992) 'Relational communication in computer-mediated interaction', *Human Communication Research*, 19(1), pp. 50–88.

Walther, J.B., Van Der Heide, B., Kim, S., Westerman, D. and Tong, S.T. (2008) 'The role of friends' appearance and behavior on evaluations of individuals on Facebook: Are we known by the company we keep?', *Human Communication Research*, 34(1), pp. 28–49.

Weber, M. (1968 [1922]) *Economy and Society: An Outline of Interpretive Sociology*. New York: Bedminster Press.

Winkin, Y. and Leeds-Hurwitz, W. (2013) *Erving Goffman: A Critical Introduction to Media and Communication Theory*. New York: Peter Lang.

Wittgenstein, L. (1953) *Philosophical Investigations*. Oxford: Blackwell.

Zuboff, S. (2019) *The Age of Surveillance Capitalism*. New York: Public Affairs.

Zukin, S. and Torpey, J. (2020) 'Editors' introduction to the special issue on the sociology of digital technology', *Theory and Society*, 49, pp. 745–8.

INDEX